ScottForesman Science
Discover the Wonder

Series Consulting Author

David Heil
Associate Director,
Oregon Museum of Science & Industry
Portland, Oregon

Consulting Authors

Maureen Allen
Science Resource Teacher/Specialist
Irvine Unified School District
Irvine, California

Dr. Timothy Cooney
Professor of Earth Science & Science Education
Earth Science Department
University of Northern Iowa
Cedar Falls, Iowa

Dr. Angie Matamoros
Lead Science Supervisor
Broward County Schools
Ft. Lauderdale, Florida

Dr. Manuel Perry
Manager, Educational Programs
Lawrence Livermore National Laboratory
Livermore, California

Dr. Irwin Slesnick
Professor of Biology
Biology Department
Western Washington University
Bellingham, Washington

 ScottForesman

A Division of HarperCollins*Publishers*

Editorial Offices: Glenview, Illinois
Regional Offices: Sunnyvale, California • Tucker, Georgia
Glenview, Illinois • Oakland, New Jersey • Dallas, Texas

Content Consultants

Dr. Linda Berne
Department of Health Promotion
and Kinesiology
University of North Carolina
Charlotte, North Carolina

Dr. Bonnie J. Buratti
Jet Propulsion Laboratory
California Institute of Technology
Pasadena, California

Dr. Norman M. Gelfand
Physicist
Fermi National Accelerator Laboratory
Accelerator Division
Batavia, Illinois

Dr. Roger A. Pielke
Professor
Department of Atmospheric Science
Colorado State University
Fort Collins, Colorado

Dr. Harrison H. Schmitt
*Former Astronaut (Apollo 17) and
United States Senator
Geologist and Science and
Technology Consultant*
Albuquerque, New Mexico

Dr. Lisa K. Wagner
Department of Biology
Georgia Southern University
Statesboro, Georgia

Multicultural Consultants

Dr. Frank Dukepoo
Department of Biology
Northern Arizona University
Flagstaff, Arizona

Dr. Deborah A. Fortune
Department of Health Promotion
and Kinesiology
University of North Carolina
Charlotte, North Carolina

Dr. Amram Gamliel
*Educational Consultant/
Professional Writer*
Newton Center, Massachusetts

Dr. Luis A. Martinez-Perez
College of Education
Florida International University
Miami, Florida

Dr. Anthony R. Sancho
*Director of Hispanic Health
Education Center*
Southwest Regional Laboratory
Los Alamitos, California

Acknowledgments

Photographs Unless otherwise acknowledged, all photographs are the property of ScottForesman. Page abbreviations are as follows: (T)top, (C)center, (B)bottom, (L)left, (R)right, (INS)inset.

Cover Design Sheldon Cotler + Associates

Cover Background: Karen Tweedy-Homes/Earth Scenes   Magnifying Glass: Richard Chesnut   Inset: John Gerlach/Animals Animals

Page v(T) Esao Hashimoto/Animals Animals   **vi(T)** David M. Dennis/Tom Stack & Associates   **viii(T)** Phil Degginger   **ix(B)** Gerald & Buff Corsi/Tom Stack & Associates   **xiii(L)** Lawrence Migdale/Stock Boston   **xiii(R)** Mike J. Howell/Stock Boston   **xiv(T)** E. R. Degginger   **xiv(B)** NASA

Illustrations Unless otherwise acknowledged, all computer graphics by The Quarasan Group, Inc.   **Page vii** Cecile Duray-Bito   **ix** Roberta Polfus

Acknowledgments continue on page 47.

About the Cover

Furry red squirrels are the most commonly seen mammal of the Great North Woods. However, they can also be found throughout the hardwood forests of the Appalachian region, such as that shown by the fall foliage of the background photograph.

Module A

Living Things

Chapter 1

Plants and Animals A 4

Lesson 1
What body parts do animals have?
Discover Activity   A 5

Lesson 2
How do body parts help animals live?   A 6

Lesson 3
What actions help animals stay alive? Visual/Verbal   A 8

Lesson 4
How can color make things hard to see? Let's Explore   A 10

Lesson 5
How do color and shape help animals?
Visual/Verbal   A 12

Lesson 6
What parts help plants live?   A 14

Lesson 7
How do some plants store water?   A 16

Lesson 8
What helps plants grow in new places?   A 18

Lesson 9
How are seeds scattered?
Let's Solve It!   A 20

Lesson 10
Chapter Review   A 22

Chapter 2

Where Things Live A 24

Lesson 1
Where do you see plants and animals?
Discover Activity — A 25

Lesson 2
Where do plants and animals live? — A 26

Lesson 3
What lives in a water habitat? Visual/Verbal — A 28

Lesson 4
How does a habitat help living things? — A 30

Lesson 5
How can you make a habitat? Let's Explore — A 32

Lesson 6
What habitats are in a zoo? Visual/Verbal — A 34

Lesson 7
What habitat can you plan for a zoo? — A 36

Lesson 8
How many red wolves live in wildlife parks?
Let's Solve It! — A 38

Lesson 9
Chapter Review — A 40

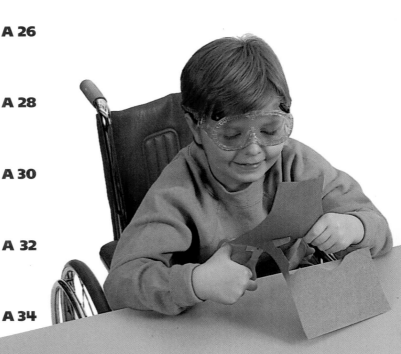

Chapter 3

Grouping Living Things A 42

Lesson 1
How can you group things? Discover Activity   A 43

Lesson 2
Is it living?   A 44

Lesson 3
How are living things grouped?   A 46

Lesson 4
What are some groups of animals? Visual/Verbal   A 48

Lesson 5
What are some kinds of body coverings?   A 50

Lesson 6
What are some other groups of animals?   A 52

Lesson 7
How can you make a model of an insect? Let's Explore   A 54

Lesson 8
How do you group plants? Let's Solve It!   A 56

Lesson 9
Chapter Review   A 58

At the end of the module
People at Work   A 60
Module Review   A 62

At the end of the book
Kids Did It   2
Study Guide   10
Experiment Skills   30

Changes Over Time

Chapter 1

Discovering Dinosaurs B 4

Lesson 1
How did dinosaurs look?
Discover Activity B 5

Lesson 2
How big were dinosaurs? B 6

Lesson 3
How long were some dinosaurs? Let's Explore B 8

Lesson 4
What did dinosaurs eat? B 10

Lesson 5
How were dinosaurs named? Visual/Verbal B 12

Lesson 6
How fast did dinosaurs move? B 14

Lesson 7
How are dinosaurs alike and different?
Let's Solve It! B 16

Lesson 8
Chapter Review B 18

Chapter 2
Dinosaur Detectives B 20

Lesson 1
What can objects tell about a person? Discover Activity **B 21**

Lesson 2
How do we learn about dinosaurs? **B 22**

Lesson 3
How can you make a fossil? Let's Explore **B 24**

Lesson 4
How do fossils form? **B 26**

Lesson 5
How do we get fossils? **B 28**

Lesson 6
What can dinosaur fossils show? Visual/Verbal **B 30**

Lesson 7
How do dinosaur bones fit together? **B 32**

Lesson 8
What else can fossils show? **B 34**

Lesson 9
What was life like long ago? Visual/Verbal **B 36**

Lesson 10
How can you measure fossils? Let's Solve It! **B 38**

Lesson 11
Chapter Review **B 40**

Chapter 3
A Changing World B 42

Lesson 1
What happened to dinosaurs?
Discover Activity   **B 43**

Lesson 2
How did dinosaurs disappear?   **B 44**

Lesson 3
What else became extinct?   **B 46**

Lesson 4
What living things are in danger? Visual/Verbal   **B 48**

Lesson 5
What else can change living things?
Let's Explore   **B 50**

Lesson 6
How does air become polluted?   **B 52**

Lesson 7
How can people help living things?   **B 54**

Lesson 8
How do zoos help endangered animals?
Let's Solve It!   **B 56**

Lesson 9
Chapter Review   **B 58**

At the end of the module
People at Work   **B 60**
Module Review   **B 62**

At the end of the book
Kids Did It   **4**
Study Guide   **14**
Experiment Skills   **32**

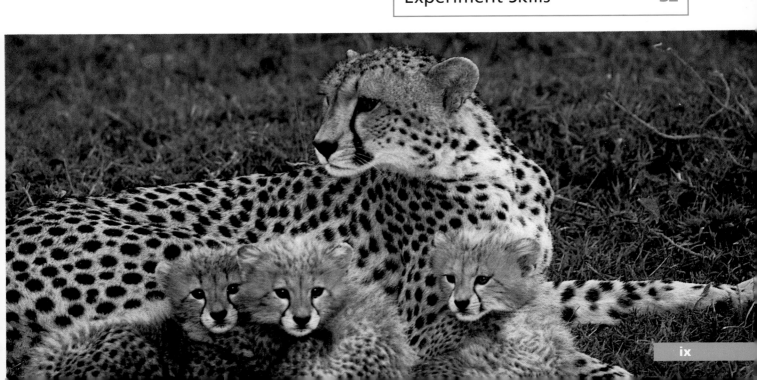

Chapter 1

How Things Move C 4

Lesson 1
How can you make a boat move?
Discover Activity   C 5

Lesson 2
What makes things move?   C 6

Lesson 3
Where are the pushes and pulls? **Visual/Verbal**   C 8

Lesson 4
How can you move something farther?   C 10

Lesson 5
What do different forces do?   C 12

Lesson 6
How does force move heavy things? **Let's Explore** C 14

Lesson 7
Where is it easier to pull things? C 16

Lesson 8
What surfaces make moving things easier?
Let's Solve It! C 18

Lesson 9
Chapter Review C 20

Chapter 2

Magnets C 22

Lesson 1
What can magnets do to each other?
Discover Activity C 23

Lesson 2
What are the poles of a magnet? C 24

Lesson 3
What can magnets do to other things? Let's Explore C 26

Lesson 4
How do you use magnets?
Visual/Verbal C 28

Lesson 5
What can a magnet pull through? Let's Explore C 30

Lesson 6
Are all magnets strong? C 32

Lesson 7
How can you make a magnet? C 34

Lesson 8
How can you make a stronger magnet?
Let's Solve It! C 36

Lesson 9
Chapter Review C 38

Chapter 3

Moving and Machines C 40

Lesson 1
What is the easiest way to move a box?
Discover Activity   **C 41**

Lesson 2
What is a machine?   **C 42**

Lesson 3
How can a ramp help move things?   **C 44**

Lesson 4
How can a lever help move things?   **C 46**

Lesson 5
How do ball bearings help move things? Let's Explore **C 48**

Lesson 6
How are body parts like a machine?   **C 50**

Lesson 7
How do you move?
Visual/Verbal   **C 52**

Lesson 8
How do muscles work?
Let's Explore   **C 54**

Lesson 9
How many bones do body parts have? Let's Solve It! **C 56**

Lesson 10
Chapter Review   **C 58**

At the end of the module
| People at Work | **C 60** |
| Module Review | **C 62** |

At the end of the book
Kids Did It	6
Study Guide	18
Experiment Skills	34

Module D

The Earth and Sky

Chapter 1

The Sun D 4

Lesson 1
How are day and night different? Discover Activity   D 5

Lesson 2
How does day turn into night? Visual/Verbal   D 6

Lesson 3
How big is the sun?   D 8

Lesson 4
What is the sun?   D 10

Lesson 5
How does sunlight help plants grow? Let's Explore   D 12

Lesson 6
How does the sun help animals?   D 14

Lesson 7
How can you use sunlight?   D 16

Lesson 8
How do coal and oil come from sunlight?   D 18

Lesson 9
How fast can you cook food in a solar oven?
Let's Solve It!   D 20

Lesson 10
Chapter Review   D 22

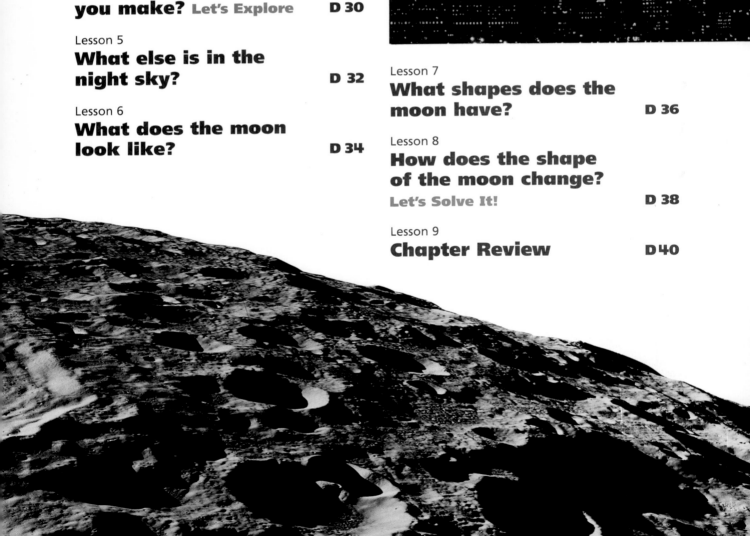

Chapter 2

The Moon and Stars D 24

Lesson 1
What does the night sky look like? Discover Activity   D 25

Lesson 2
How are other stars like the sun?   D 26

Lesson 3
How are stars grouped?
Visual/Verbal   D 28

Lesson 4
What star group can you make? Let's Explore   D 30

Lesson 5
What else is in the night sky?   D 32

Lesson 6
What does the moon look like?   D 34

Lesson 7
What shapes does the moon have?   D 36

Lesson 8
How does the shape of the moon change?
Let's Solve It!   D 38

Lesson 9
Chapter Review   D 40

Chapter 3
Looking at the Earth D 42

Lesson 1
What parts of the earth can you find?
Discover Activity   **D 43**

Lesson 2
What makes up the earth?   **D 44**

Lesson 3
What is soil like?
Let's Explore   **D 46**

Lesson 4
What are different kinds of land?   **D 48**

Lesson 5
Where is water on the earth? Visual/Verbal   **D 50**

Lesson 6
How are salt water and fresh water different?   **D 52**

Lesson 7
What is around the earth?   **D 54**

Lesson 8
Does the sun heat things the same way?
Let's Solve It!   **D 56**

Lesson 9
Chapter Review   **D 58**

At the end of the module
People at Work   **D 60**
Module Review   **D 62**

At the end of the book
Kids Did It   8
Study Guide   22
Using Scientific Methods   26
Safety in Science   28
Experiment Skills   36
Glossary/Index   38

Living Things

Living Things

How can an animal be like a plant? Animals and plants look different. But animals and plants are alike in an important way. They are living things.

Chapter 1

Plants and Animals

It can be fun to learn about different kinds of animals and plants! How do animals and plants get the things they need to stay alive? Page **A 4**

Chapter 2
Where Things Live
Each animal and plant lives in its own special place. Where do some animals and plants you know about live? Page **A 24**

Chapter 3
Grouping Living Things
You can sort objects into groups by color or shape or size. Can you sort animals and plants into groups too?
Page **A 42**

In this module

People at Work	**A 60**
Module Review	**A 62**

At the end of the book

Kids Did It	2
Study Guide	10
Using Scientific Methods	26
Safety in Science	28
Experiment Skills	30
Glossary/Index	38

Chapter 1
Plants and Animals

Did you ever wish that you could be a different animal for a day? You might like to be a bird. What kind of bird would you be?

How would you look if you were a bird? You might have bright blue feathers. Or you could have webbed feet.

What other special body parts might you have? What things could you do that you can't do now?

What body parts do animals have?

1. Find a picture of an animal in a book.

2. Look at the animal in your picture. Tell what you see.

3. Draw the body parts that you see.

4. **Tell about it.** Tell how you and the animal are alike. Tell how you and the animal are different.

Ask me what else I want to find out about animals.

How do body parts help animals live?

You just found out that animals have many kinds of body parts. These body parts can help animals stay alive. Here is how body parts help a butterfly stay alive.

Look at the big wings of this butterfly. Wings help it fly to flowers. Flowers hold a sweet food called nectar. Some butterflies eat nectar.

The butterfly has two large eyes and two long antennas. The eyes help the butterfly see flowers. The antennas help the butterfly touch and smell the flowers.

The butterfly has six legs. It uses its legs to hold onto the flower. The butterfly has a mouth like a long tube. It uses its mouth to sip nectar from a flower.

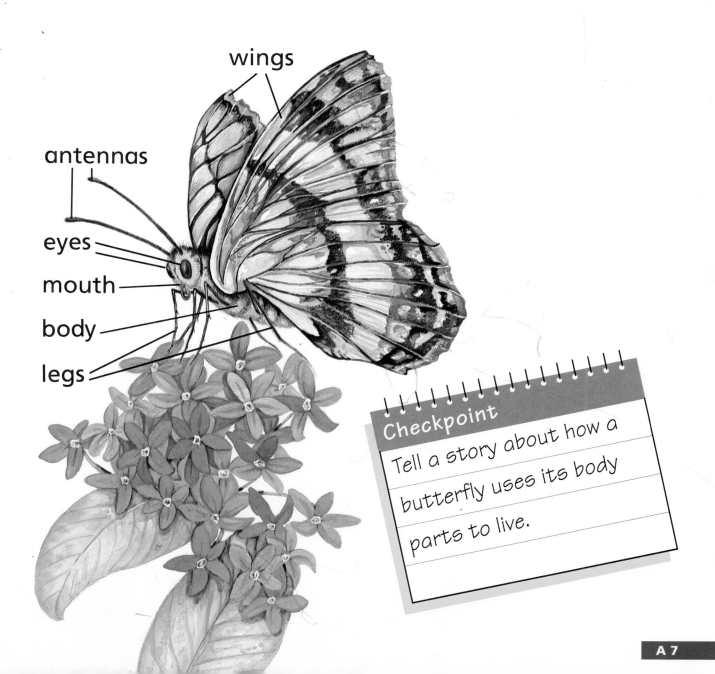

wings

antennas

eyes

mouth

body

legs

Checkpoint

Tell a story about how a butterfly uses its body parts to live.

What actions help animals stay alive?

What do animals do when they hear a noise? A bird may fly away. A squirrel may run and hide.

Animals have ways of acting that help them stay alive. A noise may be a sign of danger. Running away may help an animal get away from danger. The pictures tell about other ways of acting.

A muskrat builds its home in a pond. Other animals cannot reach it.

A squirrel buries acorns. Later it digs them up and eats them.

Checkpoint

Tell about a way of acting that helps an animal.

A duck hides her eggs from other animals.

A woodchuck **hibernates** in winter. It hardly moves. It needs very little food.

How can color make things hard to see?

Could a bird see a brown caterpillar crawling on a brown twig? You can find out how color can make things hard to see.

You will need:

○ white paper circles

● brown paper circles

 brown paper

 timer

Find out about it.

1 Get 20 white circles and 20 brown circles.

2 Have your partner place all the circles on brown paper.

3 Have your partner start the timer.

4 Use one hand. Pick up as many circles as you can in 10 seconds. Pick up one circle at a time.

5 Count the white circles you picked up. Count the brown circles you picked up.

Write about it. ✏️

Make a chart like this. Write the number of circles you picked up.

colors	circles picked up
white	
brown	

Checkpoint

1. Which color was harder to find?

2. Take Action! Draw a picture of an animal. Use color to make the animal hard to see.

How do color and shape help animals?

Think about a green caterpillar on a green leaf. Its color matches the place where it lives. Its color makes the caterpillar hard to see.

A color or shape that makes an animal hard to see is **camouflage.** Camouflage can hide an animal from other animals that might eat it. Find the animals in the pictures. How does camouflage hide each animal?

Checkpoint

Write a story about how camouflage helps animals.

deer

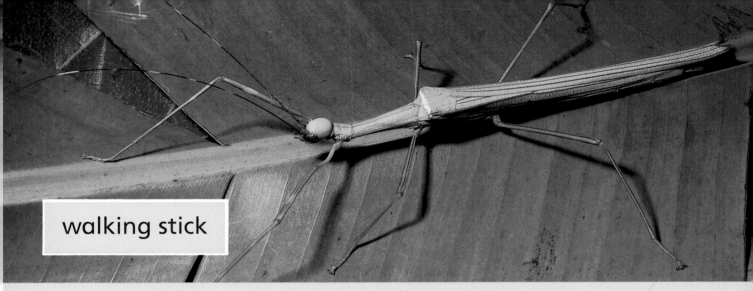

walking stick

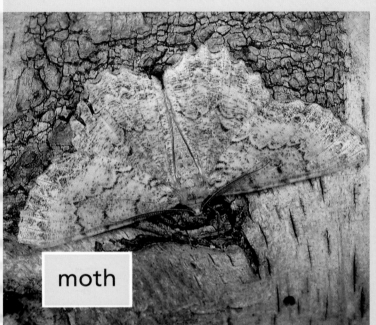

moth

hornworm

tree frogs

What parts help plants live?

Pretend you are walking on this city sidewalk. You notice trees and other plants. Plants have roots that grow under the ground. The roots help hold plants in the soil.

Roots take in water from the soil. Plants need water to live. Roots help keep trees and other plants alive.

Find the trunk of this tree. It holds up the heavy branches. The trunk is a thick stem. Stems carry water from the roots to other parts of plants.

Now find the leaves on the tree. Leaves use sunlight to help make food for plants.

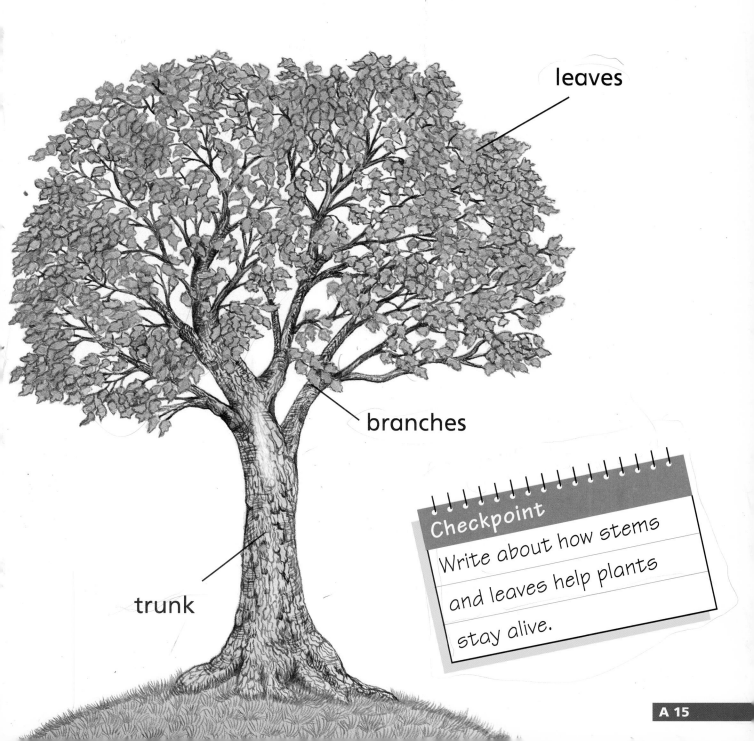

leaves

branches

trunk

Checkpoint

Write about how stems and leaves help plants stay alive.

How do some plants store water?

Suppose you live in a place that gets very little rain. You might see a cactus growing in such a dry place.

Look at the thick stems of a cactus. The stems hold water for a long time. The stored water helps the cactus grow in the desert.

Other plants store water in their leaves. Now let's see how thick leaves hold water.

Observe how plants store water.

You will need: potted jade plant

 potted fern plant water

1. Place the plants next to each other.
2. Water each plant. Make sure each plant gets the same amount of water.
3. Do not water either plant again.
4. Watch the plants until you see a change.
5. Touch the leaves carefully. Look for changes in the leaves.

Checkpoint

Tell how you know which plant stored more water. Which plant would grow better in a dry place?

What helps plants grow in new places?

Do you ever blow on a dandelion? You may like watching the dandelion fruits float through the air. When fruits float through the air, the seeds inside are scattered. Scattering helps carry the seeds to new places where they can grow. You can show how seeds are scattered through the air.

Show how seeds are scattered.

You will need: cotton balls construction paper

1. Place the paper on the floor.
2. Pull a small piece from a cotton ball.
3. Stand over the paper. Hold your arm out straight from your shoulder. Drop the cotton piece.
4. Do this ten times.
5. Watch where the pieces of cotton fall.

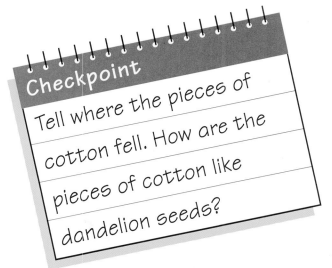

Checkpoint

Tell where the pieces of cotton fell. How are the pieces of cotton like dandelion seeds?

How are seeds scattered?

Many seeds are inside fruits. Some fruits have parts like wings or hooks. Wings help seeds be scattered by wind. Hooks help seeds be scattered by animals. The hooks can stick to animal fur. When the animal moves the fruits and seeds are carried to new places.

1. Fruit A has a part like a wing. It might be scattered by wind. Fruit B has hooks. It might be scattered by animals. Look at the other fruits. How might the parts help the seeds be scattered?

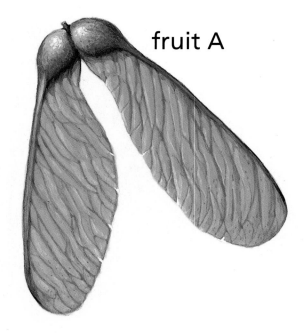

fruit A

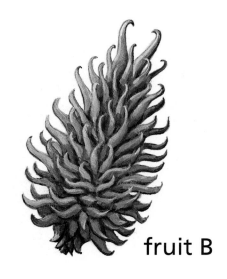

fruit B

2. Make a chart like this one.

fruit	how it looks	wings or hooks	how scattered
fruit A	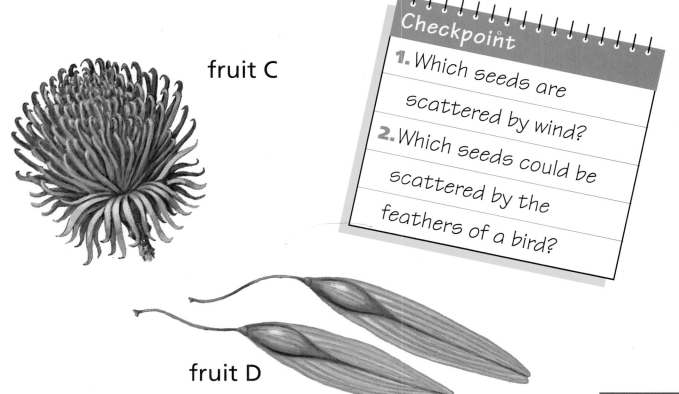	wings	wind
fruit B			
fruit C			
fruit D			

3. The chart shows fruit A. It shows its parts. It shows how the fruits and seeds are scattered. Fill in the chart for fruit B, fruit C, and fruit D.

fruit C

fruit D

Checkpoint
1. Which seeds are scattered by wind?
2. Which seeds could be scattered by the feathers of a bird?

What did you learn?

Now you know that body parts and ways of acting help animals stay alive. You also know that special parts help plants grow. You can pretend you are a plant or an animal. Then you can play a game.

You will need: paper pencil

Play a guessing game.

1. Work with a group. Make a list of plants and animals.

2. Decide who will take the part of each plant and each animal.

3. Write the name of the plant or animal on a piece of paper.

4. Write down what parts or ways of acting help your plant or animal stay alive.

5. Act out the part of your plant or animal.

6. Ask the class to guess your plant or animal.

Share what you learned.

1. How easy was it to guess what your classmates were pretending to be?
2. What was your favorite animal in the game?

Chapter 2
Where Things Live

Pretend you have a pen pal. You want to tell your pen pal about your home. What can you tell about the place where you live?

You might want to write about your neighborhood too. What can you tell about it? You can tell how it looks. You can tell about the plants and animals that live there. What kinds of places do plants and animals live in? Let's take a look!

Discover Activity

Where do you see plants and animals?

1 Cut out pictures of places where plants and animals live.

2 Glue each picture on a paper.

3 Write the names of plants and animals that live in each place.

4 **Tell about it.** Write a story about one kind of place where plants and animals live.

Ask me what else I want to find out about where plants and animals live.

Where do plants and animals live?

The place where a plant or animal lives is a **habitat.** Different plants and animals live in different kinds of habitats.

What can you tell about a habitat? You can tell how a habitat looks. You can tell how warm or cold it is. Think about other things to tell about a habitat. Then tell about the habitat in the picture.

Make a habitat for a plant.

You will need: paper cup stones
 plant 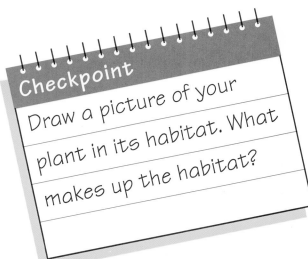 water  soil

1. Put stones in the bottom of your cup. Add soil to your cup.
2. Put your plant in the cup. Cover the roots with soil.
3. Add water to the cup.
4. Put your plant in a sunny place.

Checkpoint

Draw a picture of your plant in its habitat. What makes up the habitat?

What lives in a water habitat?

It is time for a habitat adventure. You can find out about a water habitat. Get ready to explore the pond in the picture!

You row your boat across the water. You look around. What plants do you see? What animals do you see? What can you tell about the habitat of each plant and animal?

Checkpoint

Pretend you are a plant or animal that lives in a water habitat. Tell about the habitat.

water strider

duck

dragonfly

pond habitat

turtle

How does a habitat help living things?

What do plants and animals get from their habitats? They get everything they need to live. Animals get food and water from their habitats. This spider catches insects in a web. The spider gets food and water from eating the insects.

Animals get the air they need from their habitats. They get a place to live. Animals may also get shelter to protect them from weather or danger.

What else do you see in this garden? You can see that plants live in the garden too.

The plants get sunlight. Plants get water from the soil. They get air. Plants use water, sunlight, and air to make the food they need. The garden habitat has everything the plants need to live.

Checkpoint

Tell a story about a plant or animal that lives in a garden. Tell what the plant or animal gets from its habitat.

How can you make a habitat?

Crickets and other animals need food and water. What else do crickets need to live? How can you make a habitat for crickets?

You will need:

 large box

 leaves

 soil

 food

 sticks

 2 crickets

 dropper of water

 jar lid

Find out about it.

1 Put soil in the bottom of the box.

2 Add the sticks and leaves to the box. The crickets use sticks and leaves for shelter.

3 Put the food in the box. Put water in the jar lid. Put the lid in the box.

4 Put the crickets in the box.

5 Observe the crickets.

Write about it.

Make a chart like this. Write or draw what you found out about a habitat for crickets.

what crickets need	what habitat has
food	
water	
shelter	

Checkpoint

1. What did the crickets get from the habitat you made?

2. Take Action! Draw a picture of the crickets in the habitat you made.

What habitats are in a zoo?

You see monkeys swinging from trees. You watch seals splashing in water. Where are you? You are visiting the zoo.

Many animals live at the zoo. People who work at the zoo give food and water to the animals. Look at the zoo habitats of these animals. Each animal gets everything it needs from its zoo habitat.

Checkpoint

Draw or paint a picture that shows an animal in a zoo habitat.

monkey

tiger

panda

giraffe

What habitat can you plan for a zoo?

Look in this tree. Tell about the animal you see. It is a koala. The tree is its habitat. How does this koala get everything it needs?

The koala gets food and water from eating leaves. It gets shelter from the tree.

Pretend you work in a zoo. Your job is to make a habitat for a koala.

Make a model of a zoo habitat.

You will need: cover goggles shoe box

 construction paper crayons glue

 scissors pipe cleaners

1. Draw a picture of a koala. Cut out your picture.
2. Make a habitat for the koala in your shoe box.
3. Put your koala in its habitat.

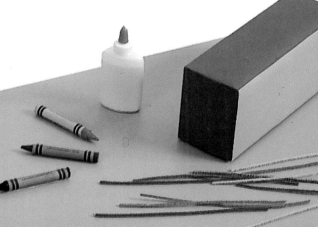

Checkpoint

Do a radio show. Tell about the new zoo habitat for the koala. Invite people to come to the zoo.

How many red wolves live in wildlife parks?

Sometimes red wolves cannot live in their habitat. Some of these red wolves are sent to live in wildlife parks. These habitats have everything the red wolves need to live.

1. Look at the pictures. You can see that 20 red wolves were sent to habitat A. How many wolves went to each of the other habitats?

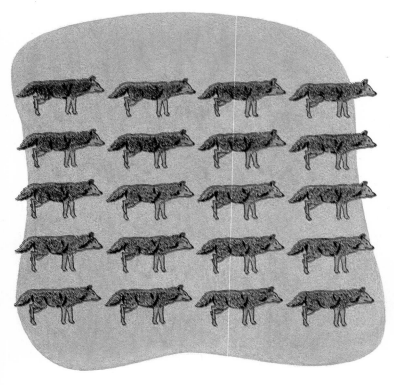

habitat A

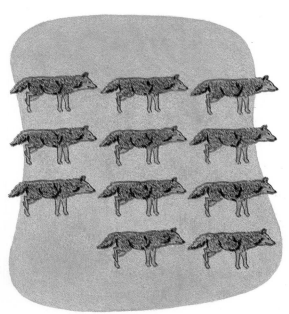

habitat B

2. Draw a chart like this one.

habitat	number of wolves
habitat A	20
habitat B	
habitat C	

3. The chart shows how many red wolves live in habitat A. Fill in the chart for habitats B and C.

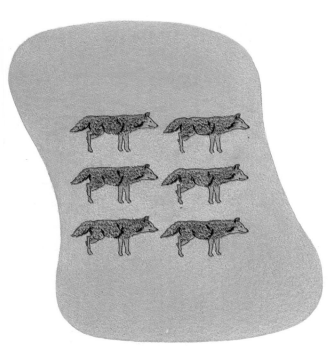

habitat C

Checkpoint

1. Which habitat has the most red wolves?

2. How many red wolves were sent to habitats B and C?

What did you learn?

You learned what plants and animals get from their habitats. Now make a habitat book. Show a habitat for a plant or animal. Then tell about the habitat.

You will need: crayons paper  pencil

Make a book about a habitat.

1. Draw a picture of a plant or animal on your paper.
2. Add a habitat for the plant or animal to your picture.
3. Write a story on another paper. Tell what the plant or animal needs to live.
4. Make a cover for your book.
5. Put the pages inside the cover.

A 41

Share what you learned.

1. Can other plants and animals live in your habitat?
2. What can you tell about a habitat near your school?

Chapter 3

Grouping Living Things

Look at all these shoes! Do any of them look like yours? Do any of them look alike? Things that are alike can be grouped together.

Now look around your classroom. Find more shoes. How could you group these shoes?

How can you group things?

1 Draw your favorite shoe.

2 Color the shoe. Then cut it out.

3 Sit in a circle with five classmates. Put your shoe picture in the center of the circle.

4 Find the shoes that are the same color. Put them in a group.

5 Group the shoes in other ways. Try grouping them by size or shape.

6 **Tell about it.** Write down how the shoes in each group are alike.

Ask me what else I want to find out about grouping things.

Is it living?

Pretend you are taking a walk. You might see a bird. You might see grass. How are the bird and the grass alike? They are **living things.** Living things can grow.

What other things do you see? You might see a building. You might see a rock. Buildings and rocks are **nonliving things.** They do not grow. What other nonliving things might you see?

Group living and nonliving things.

You will need: magazines ✂ scissors

1. Look at the pictures in the magazines.
2. Cut out pictures of living things. Cut out pictures of nonliving things.
3. Put pictures of living things in a group. Put pictures of nonliving things in a group.

Checkpoint

Tell a story about one of your pictures.

How are living things grouped?

Pretend you are visiting a park. You see living things in the park. How can you group these living things?

You can put the chipmunk, bird, and the ladybug into one group. How are they alike? They are animals. Most animals can move from place to place. Animals eat the food they find in their habitats.

You can put the grass and the trees into another group. How are grass and trees alike? They are plants. Plants cannot move from one place to another. Plants use sunlight to make the food they need.

Checkpoint

Write a commercial for a new park. Tell what groups of living things people can see in the park.

What are some groups of animals?

Imagine walking into this pet store. There are so many animals to see!

First find the animals that live in water. Did you find the fish? Now look for the birds. How are they alike? Notice that animals that are alike are grouped together. Find other groups of animals in the picture.

Checkpoint

Draw a picture of an animal. Write the name of the group the animal belongs to.

Canaries belong to a group called **birds.**

Turtles belong to a group called **reptiles.**

CHEWING TOYS

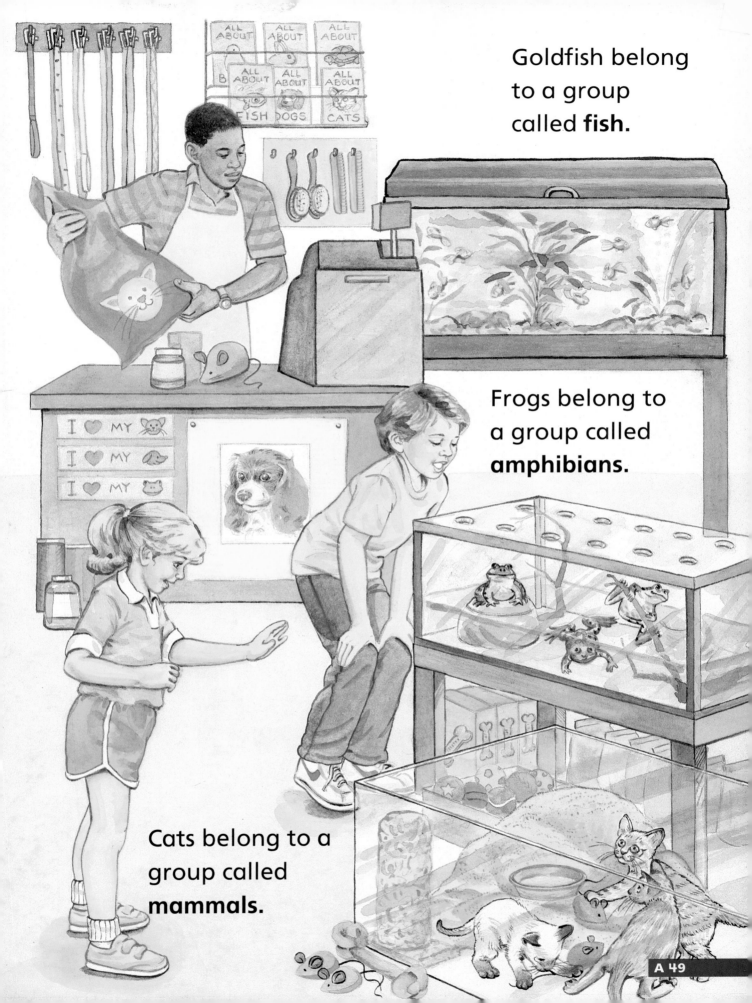

Goldfish belong to a group called **fish.**

Frogs belong to a group called **amphibians.**

Cats belong to a group called **mammals.**

What are some kinds of body coverings?

Imagine petting this soft, furry puppy. A puppy is a mammal. Mammals have hair or fur covering their bodies. Do other kinds of animals feel furry? Reptiles have rough, dry skin. Amphibians have smooth, wet skin.

Birds have feathers covering their bodies. Most fish have scales covering their bodies. What are feathers and scales like?

Observe body coverings.

You will need:  bird feather ⬭ hand lens

🐟 fish scales ▢ paper ✏ pencil

1. Look at the feather with the hand lens. Draw what you see.
2. Touch the feather. Feel the different parts. Write down how the feather feels.
3. Look at the fish scales with the hand lens. Draw what you see.
4. Touch the fish scales. Write down how the scales feel.

Checkpoint

Write a story about an animal. Tell about its body covering.

What are some other groups of animals?

Pretend you are digging in this soil. You find a worm. You look at it. The worm has a long soft body. It does not have legs. You watch the worm crawl around the ground. The worm in this picture lives in soil. Other worms live in water.

You see an ant on a nearby flower. Ants belong to a group of animals called **insects.** Ants and other insects have three main body parts. Insects have six legs. Many ants do not have wings. Insects such as bees do have wings.

You find other animals on the ground. You see a spider. It has two main body parts. You notice that the spider does not have wings. You count eight legs on the spider.

Checkpoint

Draw a picture of a spider. Show the body parts of the spider.

How can you make a model of an insect?

Suppose you see an insect on your way to school. You want to tell a classmate about the insect. One way to tell about the insect is to make a model.

You will need:

 cover goggles

 picture of an insect

 clay

 paper

 pipe cleaners

 scissors

 glue

Find out about it.

1 Get a picture of an insect from your teacher. Look closely at the picture.

2 Make the main body parts of the insect out of pieces of clay. Use pipe cleaners to put the parts together.

3 Make legs from pipe cleaners.

4 Put the legs on the body of the insect.

5 Add other parts your insect might have.

Write about it.

Make a chart like this one. Write down
how many parts your model has.

kind of part	how many parts
main body parts	
legs	
wings	
antennas	
eyes	

Checkpoint

1. What kind of insect did you make?

2. Take Action! See how your model is different from a model made by a classmate.

How do you group plants?

Pretend you are looking at plants with flowers. You see veins in the leaves.

The veins of some leaves are in straight lines. The veins of other leaves spread out like a web.

1. Look at the pictures. Leaf A has veins that are spread out. Leaf B has veins that are in straight lines. How do the veins in leaf C and leaf D look?

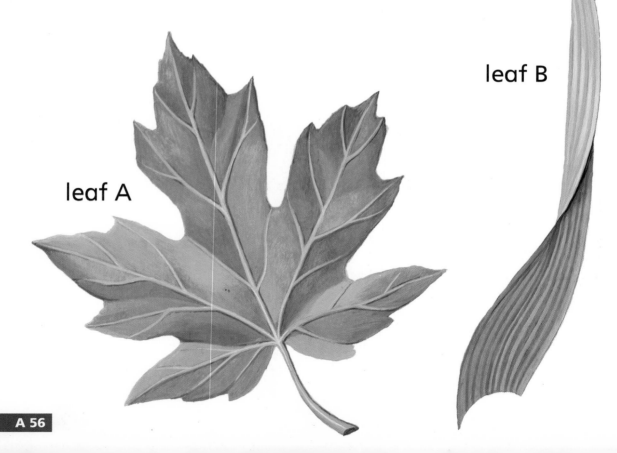

leaf A

leaf B

2. Make a chart like this one.

leaf	how leaf looks	veins in straight lines	veins that spread out
leaf A	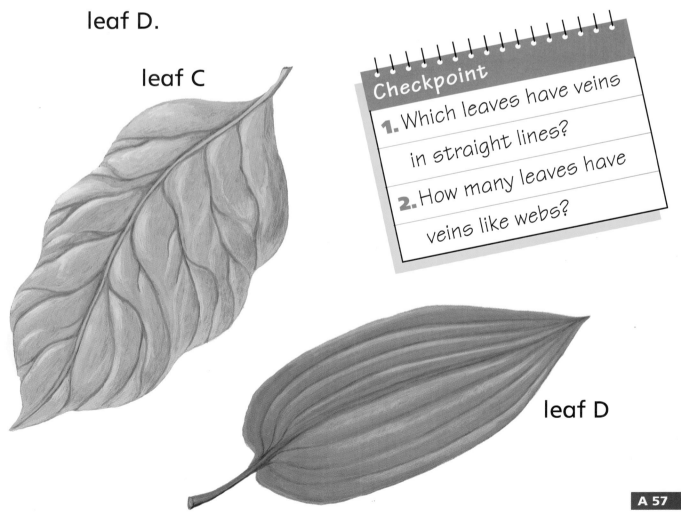		X
leaf B		X	
leaf C			
leaf D			

3. The chart tells about the veins in leaf A and leaf B. Fill in the chart for leaf C and leaf D.

leaf C

leaf D

Checkpoint

1. Which leaves have veins in straight lines?

2. How many leaves have veins like webs?

What did you learn?

You can match living and nonliving things with words that tell about them.

You will need: ☐ note cards ✏ pencil

Play a matching game.

1. Get 8 note cards from your teacher.
2. Write 8 things from this list on your notecards.

worm	nonliving
bird	plant
spider	long, soft body
fish	veins
insect	feathers
building	8 legs
tree	scales
leaf	6 legs

3. Tell your partner to write the 8 other things on note cards.

4. Put all the cards face down on the table.
5. Turn one card over.
6. Pick up another card to match the first card. Turn the card face down if it is not a match.
7. Play until a match is made. Keep the matched cards face up on the table.
8. Take turns until all the cards are matched.

Share what you learned.

1. What 2 cards did you match first?
2. What kinds of animals do you see on your way to school? What words tell about the animals?

A visit to a pet store

Imagine visiting a pet store. You see rabbits sleeping. You hear birds singing. You watch fish swimming in aquariums. What else might you see?

Pet store workers take care of the animals. The workers make sure the animals stay healthy. The workers clean the cages. They clean the aquariums. Pet store workers give the animals food and water every day.

How does an aquarium work?

1 The air pump puts air into the water.

2 The filter keeps the water clean.

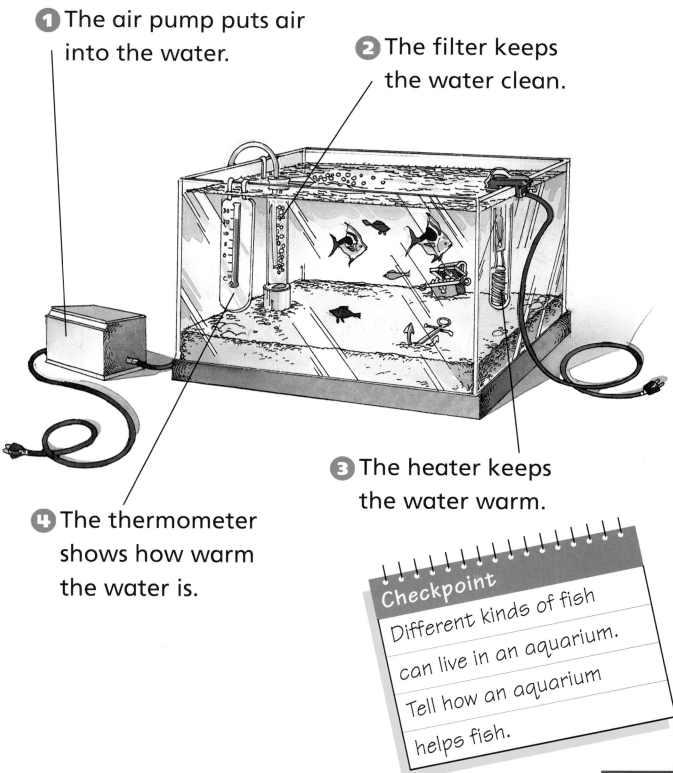

3 The heater keeps the water warm.

4 The thermometer shows how warm the water is.

Checkpoint

Different kinds of fish can live in an aquarium.

Tell how an aquarium helps fish.

Show what you know.

Suppose you want to tell about one animal or plant. You can tell how it looks. You can tell about its habitat. What else can you tell? Choose an animal or plant you want to tell about. Have a nature show to tell others about your plant or animal.

Plan your nature show.

1. Pick a project you would like to do.
2. Get what you need to do your project.
3. What will you do first?
4. Think about how you will tell about your animal or plant.

Make a mobile.

Draw a big picture of your plant or animal. Draw pictures about your plant or animal on note cards. Tape yarn to each card. Tape the cards to the big picture. Hang your mobile!

Put on a play.

Pretend to be an animal or plant. Act out what your animal or plant does. Show other things about your animal or plant. See if your classmates can guess what you are.

Give a report.

Write a report about your animal or plant. Draw pictures that go with your report. Give your report to your class.

Share what you know.

1. Show others what you have done.
2. What did you like the most about the way your project turned out?

Changes Over Time

Changes Over Time

The world of long ago looked much different from the world you live in today. The earth is always changing. Changes happen to animals and plants too.

Discovering Dinosaurs

What were dinosaurs really like? You might be surprised to find out how many kinds of dinosaurs lived. Page **B 4**

Chapter 2

Dinosaur Detectives

Dinosaurs do not live on the earth any more. How do people know so much about dinosaurs and the way they lived? Page **B 20**

Chapter 3

A Changing World

Even a small change on the earth can make a difference to plants and animals. What kinds of changes can help animals and plants? Page **B 42**

In this module

People at Work	**B 60**
Module Review	**B 62**

At the end of the book

Kids Did It	4
Study Guide	14
Using Scientific Methods	26
Safety in Science	28
Experiment Skills	32
Glossary/Index	38

Chapter 1
Discovering Dinosaurs

Pretend you are on a trip to the past. You go back a long time ago. You visit the world in the picture. No people were living then. But dinosaurs lived in many places on the earth. What were dinosaurs really like? Let's take a closer look!

How did dinosaurs look?

1 Make a model of a dinosaur. Shape the body and the legs.

2 Make a tail on your model.

3 Add eyes and teeth to your dinosaur.

4 **Tell about it.** Write a story about your dinosaur. What does it eat? How does it move? What is its name?

Ask me what else I want to find out about dinosaurs.

How big were dinosaurs?

Were all dinosaurs giants? The answer may surprise you. Dinosaurs were many sizes.

The biggest dinosaur in the picture was taller than most school buildings. This dinosaur was heavy too. It was heavier than ten elephants.

Imagine standing next to the middle dinosaur in the picture. It was about the size of a school bus. You would not even reach its knee!

Brachiosaurus

You would be taller than the small dinosaur in the picture. This dinosaur was only about the size of a chicken.

Checkpoint

Draw a picture of a dinosaur next to another object. Let your picture show how big your dinosaur is.

Allosaurus

Compsognathus

How long were some dinosaurs?

Could dinosaurs have fit in your classroom? You might guess that some dinosaurs could have fit in it. You can use a string to find out how long some dinosaurs were.

You will need:

 string

 masking tape

 meter stick

Find out about it.

1. Stretch out the string your teacher gives you.

2. Find an object in your classroom as long as your string.

3. Tape one end of the string to each end of the object.

4. Measure the string.

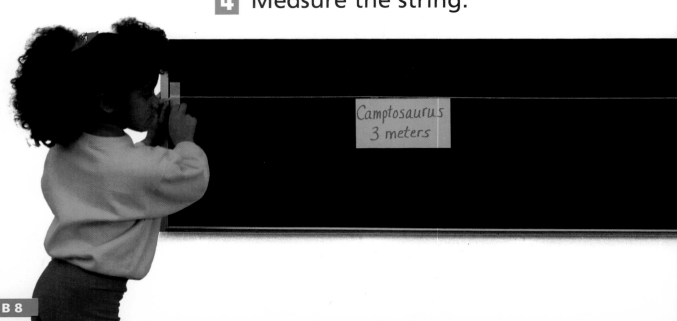

Camptosaurus
3 meters

Write about it.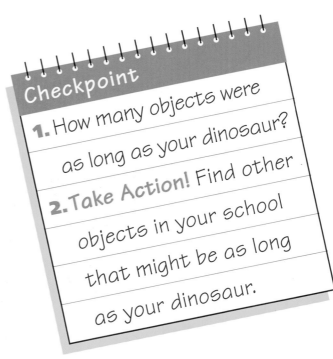

Make a chart like this. Write the name of your dinosaur. Write how long it was. Draw a picture of an object that is as long as your dinosaur.

name	how long	object

Checkpoint

1. How many objects were as long as your dinosaur?

2. Take Action! Find other objects in your school that might be as long as your dinosaur.

What did dinosaurs eat?

What are some of your favorite foods? Did dinosaurs eat the same kinds of foods you do?

Some dinosaurs had long, sharp teeth for eating meat. Other dinosaurs had big, flat teeth for eating plants. The pictures tell about the kinds of foods some dinosaurs ate.

Triceratops

Compsognathus

Tyrannosaurus

Stegosaurus

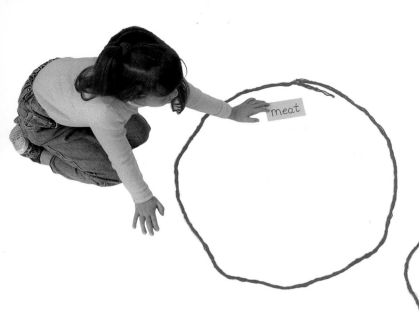

Sort dinosaurs by their foods.

You will need: yarn

 note cards  markers

1. Make a circle on the floor.
2. Write the word *meat* on a card. Put the card in the circle.
3. Make another circle with yarn.
4. Write the word *plant* on a card. Put the card in the circle.
5. Look at the dinosaurs on the last page. Write each dinosaur name on a card. Notice if each dinosaur ate meat or plants.
6. Put each card in the right circle.

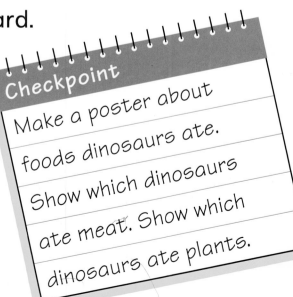

Checkpoint

Make a poster about foods dinosaurs ate. Show which dinosaurs ate meat. Show which dinosaurs ate plants.

How were dinosaurs named?

Suppose you need to name an animal. You might name the animal by the way it looks. You might name it by the way it acts.

The name dinosaur means "terrible lizard." What does the name tell about dinosaurs? Look at these dinosaurs and their names. What do names tell about the dinosaurs?

Oviraptor means "egg stealer."

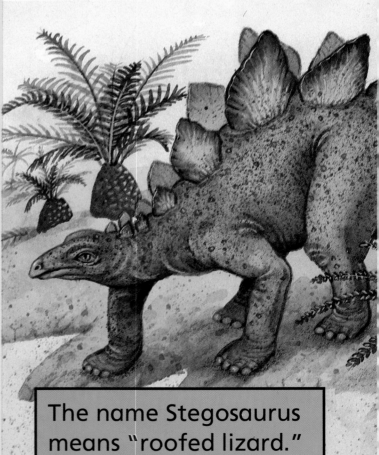

The name Stegosaurus means "roofed lizard."

Checkpoint

Paint a picture of a dinosaur. Give your dinosaur a name that tells about it.

Triceratops means
"three-horned face."

Deinonychus means
"terrible claw."

How fast did dinosaurs move?

   Did dinosaurs move slowly like turtles do? Or were they fast like tigers? You may guess that some dinosaurs moved faster than others.

   Imagine that you live in the world of dinosaurs. You watch the dinosaur in the first picture take big, slow steps. A fast runner might win a race with this dinosaur!

Apatosaurus

Suppose the dinosaur with the horns ran by. Could you catch it? No, it moved fast. It could run faster than you can ride a bicycle.

This small dinosaur was the fastest one of all. Its strong legs helped it run. It could run almost as fast as a car can move.

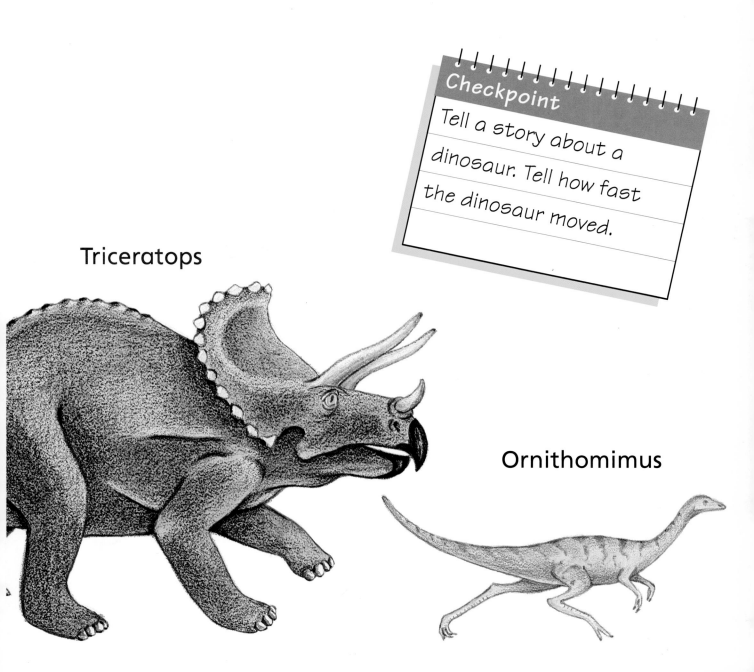

Checkpoint
Tell a story about a dinosaur. Tell how fast the dinosaur moved.

Triceratops

Ornithomimus

How are dinosaurs alike and different?

One way to compare dinosaurs is by looking at how long they were. The drawings show how long four dinosaurs were.

1. Look at the drawings of dinosaurs. Apatosaurus was the longest dinosaur. Which was the shortest dinosaur?

Tyrannosaurus
12 meters long

Stegosaurus
6 meters long

2. Draw a chart like this one.

Stegosaurus									
Apatosaurus									
Tyrannosaurus									
Iguanodon									

0   3   6   9   12   15   18   21   24

meters

3. The chart shows how long the Stegosaurus was. Color your chart to show how long the other dinosaurs were.

Checkpoint

1. Which dinosaurs were longer than the Stegosaurus?

2. Write the names of the dinosaurs in order from the shortest to the longest.

Apatosaurus
24 meters long

Iguanodon
9 meters long

What did you learn?

Look again at the dinosaur you made at the beginning of this chapter. How can you make it more like a dinosaur that really lived?

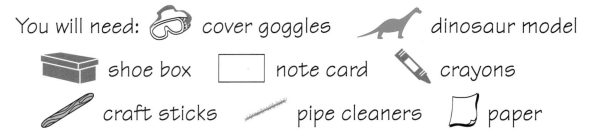

You will need: cover goggles   dinosaur model   shoe box   note card   crayons   craft sticks   pipe cleaners   paper

Make a dinosaur museum.

1. Make your dinosaur look more like a real dinosaur. You can use what you learned to change your model.

2. Use a shoe box to make a home for your dinosaur. Decorate the box to show how the land looked.

3. Make a card like the one in the picture. Write what your dinosaur was like.

4. Draw a picture of your dinosaur on the back of the card.

name
size
food.
how it walked

Share what you learned.

1. How did you change your dinosaur?
2. What does your museum show about dinosaurs?
3. What is your favorite dinosaur?

B 19

Chapter 2
Dinosaur Detectives

Can you solve this mystery? You find an object on your desk. You did not see anyone. But the object is a clue that tells you that someone was near your desk.

People have never seen dinosaurs. How do we know that they lived? We learn about dinosaurs by looking at the clues they left behind. Let's find out more.

What can objects tell about a person?

1. Take the bag your teacher gives you.
2. Look in the bag for objects that give clues about a person.
3. Study the objects. Tell what you think the person is like.
4. **Tell about it.** Think about one kind of dinosaur. List objects that might give clues about your dinosaur.

Ask me what else I want to find out about how dinosaurs lived.

How do we learn about dinosaurs?

Imagine that you are taking a walk. You step in soft, wet mud. Look! You can see your footprints. What might your footprints show about your size? What else might your footprints show about you?

Long ago, this dinosaur walked through mud. How are its footprints different from yours? What might footprints show about the dinosaur?

Tyrannosaurus

Make a shoe print.

You will need: clay plastic wrap shoe

1. Roll a piece of clay out flat. Put the piece of clay between two pieces of plastic wrap.
2. Step carefully with one foot on the clay. Take the plastic wrap off of your print.
3. Take off your shoe. Put it in a pile with those of your classmates.
4. Match the shoe prints with the shoes.

Checkpoint

Tell what your shoe print shows.

How can you make a fossil?

What happened to the footprints dinosaurs left behind? Some footprints became **fossils**. A fossil can be a part or a mark from an animal or plant. How can your clay shoe print become a fossil?

You will need:

 clay shoe print

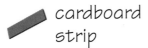 cardboard strip

 masking tape

 plaster of Paris

 plastic knife

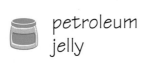 petroleum jelly

Find out about it.

1 Cut around the shoe print you made.

2 Coat the shoe print with petroleum jelly.

3 Tape the cardboard strip around your shoe print.

4 Fill the shoe print with plaster of Paris. Let it dry.

5 Take away the cardboard. Carefully peel away the clay from your fossil.

Write about it.

Make a chart like this one. Draw what your fossil shows.

what my fossil looks like

Checkpoint

1. What does your fossil show about your shoe?

2. Take Action! List the things your fossil shows about you.

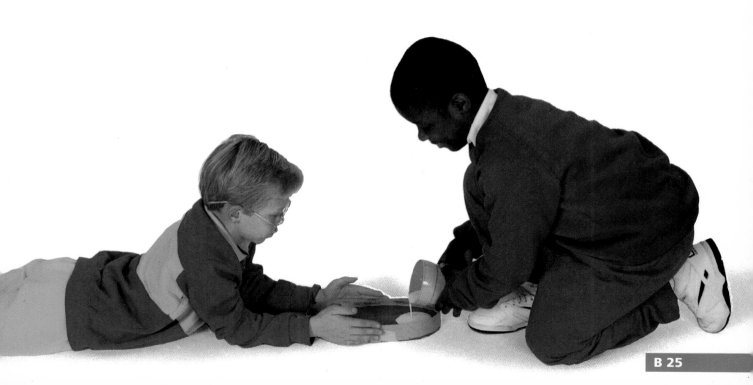

How do fossils form?

Did you ever see a mark like the one on this rock? How did the mark get there?

Long ago, an animal died. It became covered with mud. The mud dried and became hard. The body of the animal rotted away. The shell of the animal was left. Then the shell wore away. Only the animal's mark stayed in the rock. The mark had become a fossil.

If you go on a fossil hunt, you might find fossils like these. Point to the fossil that came from an animal. Point to the fossil that came from a plant. What can fossils show about animals and plants that lived long ago?

Checkpoint

Make a picture book that shows how a fossil forms.

How do we get fossils?

You pick up a handful of dirt. You know that fossils are buried in rocks and dirt. If fossils were here, how would you get them?

Digging for fossils is a hard job. Workers use tools to dig deep into the ground. These workers uncover fossils. They gently brush away some of the dirt. Workers need to be very careful not to break any fossils.

Dig for fossils.

You will need: 🥽 cover goggles   🐟 fossil

✏️ craft stick   🖌️ paintbrush

1. Study the object you get from your teacher. Find where the fossil is hidden.
2. Scratch your object until you uncover the fossil.
3. Take your fossil out and clean it.

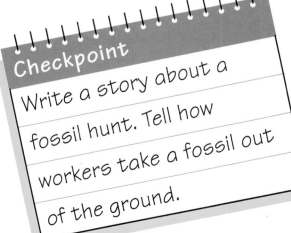

Checkpoint

Write a story about a fossil hunt. Tell how workers take a fossil out of the ground.

What can dinosaur fossils show?

Imagine finding these giant bones. You probably would ask "What kind of animal had bones like these?" These bones were from a dinosaur.

The dinosaur bones were buried in mud for many years. Slowly the mud and the bones hardened. The bones became fossils. What can these fossils show about dinosaurs?

The Iguanodon was taller than a house — and as long as a house too.

The Iguanodon probably lifted its tail when it ran.

Checkpoint

Make a model of a dinosaur bone from clay.

Tell about your bone.

Iguanodon

The Iguanodon had big, flat teeth for eating plants.

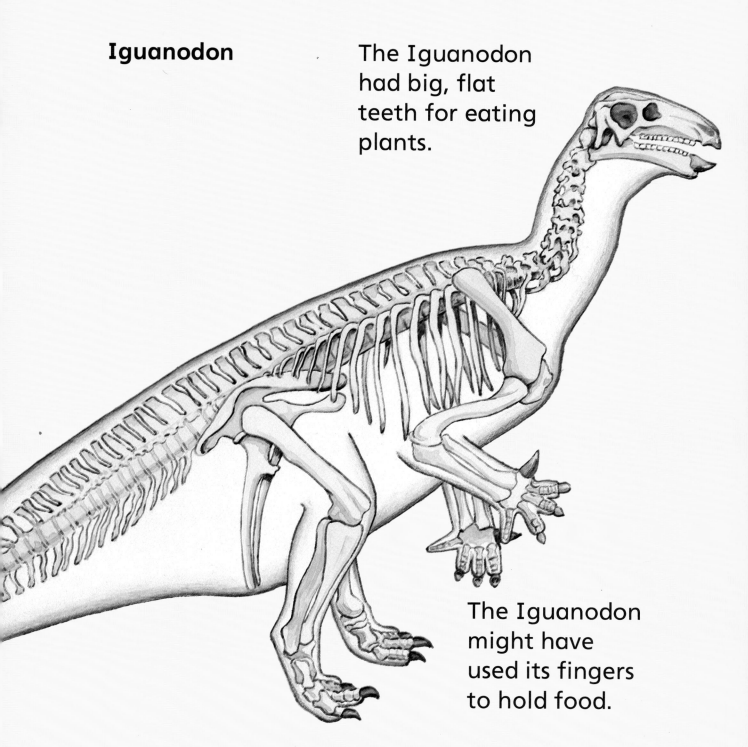

The Iguanodon might have used its fingers to hold food.

The Iguanodon probably walked on its two back legs.

How do dinosaur bones fit together?

Do you like puzzles? Suppose you have many puzzle pieces. How can you find out what the whole puzzle shows?

Fitting together dinosaur bones is like putting together a puzzle. Workers need to figure out where each bone belongs. Then they put the bones together.

Make a model of a dinosaur skeleton.

You will need: cover goggles ⟋⟍⟋ pipe cleaners

1. Twist two pipe cleaners together to make one long piece.
2. Bend one end of the long piece to make the head of the dinosaur. Bend the rest of the piece to make the back and the tail.
3. Use pipe cleaners to make front and back legs.
4. Use pipe cleaners for ribs. Twist the ribs around the back.

Checkpoint

Put on a puppet show with your dinosaur skeleton. Tell what bones can show about your dinosaur.

What else can fossils show?

Let's play a "guess the animal" game. This animal laid eggs in nests. Babies hatched from the eggs. The babies probably stayed near their nests for a long time. What animal was it? You can find the answer in the picture.

How do we know about these dinosaurs? People digging for fossils found nests. In the nests, they found pieces of eggshells. Fossils of dinosaur babies were in the nests too.

Maiasaur and babies

Fossils of young dinosaurs were near the nests. The teeth were worn from eating. How did the young dinosaurs get food? Near one nest, people found fossils of a grown dinosaur. Dinosaurs probably brought food to their babies.

Checkpoint

Act out a play about dinosaurs. Show how dinosaurs took care of their babies.

What was life like long ago?

Pretend that you peek around one of these trees. Look at the world of the dinosaurs. Does it look the way you imagined it? How is it the same? How is it different?

You may be surprised to see so many animals and plants. How do we know so much about life long ago? If you said that we learned from fossils, you are right!

Checkpoint

Make a diorama. Show some animals and plants that lived long ago.

How can you measure fossils?

You learned that many kinds of plants lived long ago. Now you might see fossils of some of these plants. You can measure these fossils.

1. Look at the fossils of the plants. The yew is the shortest fossil. Which is the tallest fossil?

fern

cycad

2. Draw a chart like this one.

fern												
cycad												
yew												

0 1 2 3 4 5 6 7 8 9 10 11 12

centimeters

3. The chart shows how tall the fern fossil is. Color your chart to show how tall the other fossils are.

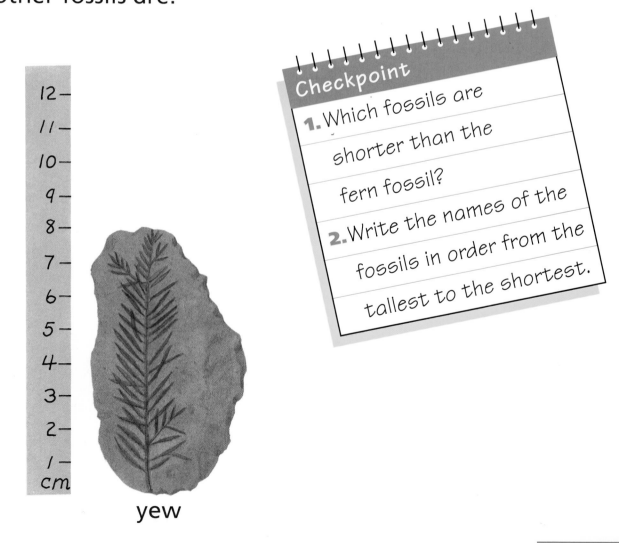

12 —
11 —
10 —
9 —
8 —
7 —
6 —
5 —
4 —
3 —
2 —
1 —
cm

yew

Checkpoint

1. Which fossils are shorter than the fern fossil?

2. Write the names of the fossils in order from the tallest to the shortest.

What did you learn?

You know that fossils tell us about animals of long ago. You found out that fossils tell about plants too. You can make a game about fossils.

You will need:  paper  crayons  scissors

Make a fossil game.

1. Draw pictures of three animals or plants from long ago.
2. Draw fossils that tell about each animal or plant.
3. Cut your pictures apart.
4. Trade pictures with a classmate.
5. Match each picture of an animal or a plant with its fossil.

Chapter 3

A Changing World

Has your neighborhood changed since last year? Maybe some new stores are being built. Maybe new neighbors have moved in. The world around you is always changing.

When dinosaurs lived, the world was changing too. But the dinosaurs were not able to live in this changing world. People have different ideas about how the world changed. Maybe you have your own ideas.

What happened to dinosaurs?

1 Draw a picture of a dinosaur on one side of a paper.

2 Draw a picture on the other side of your paper. Show what you think might have happened to the dinosaur.

3 **Tell about it.** Write a story about your dinosaur. Tell what might have happened to it.

Ask me what else I want to find out about the changing world.

NEW HOMES

MOVING CO.

How did dinosaurs disappear?

Dinosaurs lived on the earth for many years. Now dinosaurs are **extinct.** Extinct animals are kinds of animals that no longer live on the earth.

Nobody really knows what happened to dinosaurs. But the weather became colder at about the same time dinosaurs became extinct. Maybe dinosaurs could not live in the cold weather.

Many people think that a big rock from space crashed into the earth. Maybe dust from the crash blocked sunlight. Without sunlight, plants could not grow. Then dinosaurs could not live.

New kinds of animals began to live on the earth. Maybe these animals ate plants the dinosaurs needed for food. Maybe these animals even ate dinosaur eggs.

Checkpoint

Do a TV news show. Tell how you think dinosaurs became extinct.

What else became extinct?

How are the animals in the picture like dinosaurs? These kinds of animals are extinct. There are many kinds of extinct plants and animals.

Remember that a living thing gets everything it needs from its habitat. What happens when a habitat is changed? Some plants and animals may not be able to get the things they need. They become extinct.

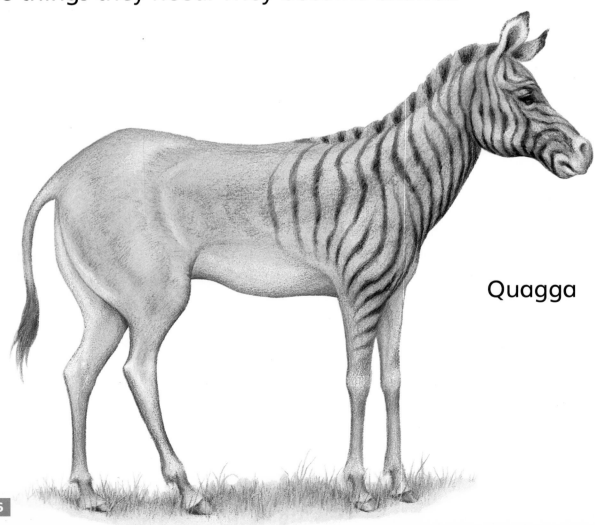

Quagga

Here is what happened to the extinct bird in the picture below. This bird once lived in grassy places. Then its habitat changed. Many trees began to grow on the land.

Many of the birds could not find the food they needed to live. After a while, the birds became extinct.

Moa

Checkpoint

Draw a picture of a plant or animal. Draw its habitat. Tell what can happen if its habitat is changed.

What living things are in danger?

Many kinds of living things are in danger of becoming extinct. These living things are **endangered.** That means that very few of these animals and plants are living. Many animals and plants become endangered when their habitats change. The plants and animals you see here are endangered.

Checkpoint

Make a poster for your classroom about an endangered plant or animal.

whooping crane

giant panda

small whorled pogonia

Hawaiian monk seal

cheetah

What else can change living things?

Living things get water from their habitats. Plants get some of this water from rain. But suppose the rain water is **polluted.** Polluted water is dirty water. Can polluted water harm a plant?

You will need:

 cover goggles

 clean water

 polluted water

 plant cuttings

Find out about it.

1 Get a cup of clean water from your teacher. Get a cup of polluted water from your teacher.

2 Look carefully at the plant cuttings.

3 Put one plant cutting into the clean water. Put the other plant cutting into the polluted water.

4 Wait a few hours. Look again at the plant cuttings.

Write about it. ✏️

Make a chart like this one. Draw what you found out.

clean water	polluted water

Checkpoint

1. What happened to the plant cuttings?

2. Take Action! Draw what might happen to plants if rain water is polluted.

clean water

polluted water

How does air become polluted?

Take in a big breath. Now let it out. You are breathing air. You need air to stay alive. Clean air is important for all living things.

Polluted air is dirty. It can harm living things. Polluted air can have dust and dirt in it. Polluted air can have smoke. Find things in the picture that can make air polluted. Can you always see what is in the air? You can find out.

Find out what is in the air.

You will need:  jar lids   petroleum jelly   paper towels   hand lens

1. Dip a paper towel in petroleum jelly.
2. Spread the petroleum jelly on the inside of two jar lids.
3. Place one lid in your classroom. Place the other lid outside.
4. Wait a few days. Use a hand lens to look at the two jar lids.

Checkpoint

Tell if the air outside has dirt in it. How do you know?

How can people help living things?

How are these people helping the earth? When you keep the earth clean, you are helping protect the habitats of living things.

How else can people help plants and animals? People can make parks. Plants and animals can live in the parks.

Here is something you can do to help living things. You can help birds get enough food.

Make a bird feeder.

You will need:  cover goggles milk carton

 crayons scissors stick

 birdseed string

1. Draw a circle on one side of the carton. Cut out the circle.
2. Put a small hole below the opening you made. Push the stick through the hole.
3. Put two holes through the top of the carton. Pull string through the holes.
4. Put birdseed in your feeder.
5. Tie the string. Hang your bird feeder outside.

Checkpoint

Tell a story about an animal or plant. Tell how people have helped it live.

How do zoos help endangered animals?

The snow leopard is endangered. People took some snow leopards to live in zoos. In zoos, snow leopards get everything they need to live. Baby snow leopards are born at zoos. The number of snow leopards is getting bigger.

1. Look at the chart. It shows about how many snow leopards were born in zoos for four years. How many snow leopards were born in zoos in 1989?

year	number of snow leopards born in zoos
1989	40
1990	30
1991	20
1992	50

2. Draw a chart like this one.

year	number of snow leopards born in zoos									
1989	░	░	░	░	░	░	░	░		
1990										
1991										
1992										

0   5   10   15   20   25   30   35   40   45   50

3. The chart shows about how many snow leopards were born in zoos in 1989. Fill in the chart for 1990, 1991, and 1992.

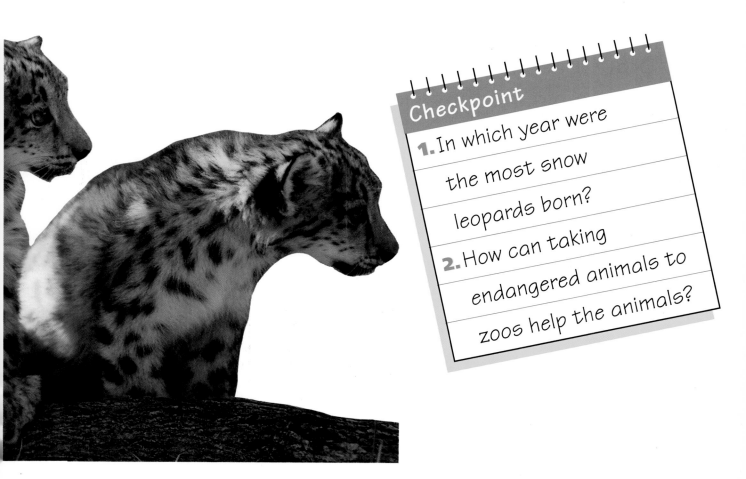

Checkpoint

1. In which year were the most snow leopards born?

2. How can taking endangered animals to zoos help the animals?

What did you learn?

You know that the world of dinosaurs changed. The world of other animals and plants changes too. You read about some of these changes. You can make a book that shows what you learned.

You will need: ▢ 4 sheets of paper ✏ pencil 🖍 crayons ◈ construction paper

Make a book.

1. Draw a picture of an extinct animal.
2. Draw an endangered animal or plant.
3. Draw a picture that shows polluted air or polluted water.
4. Draw a picture of one way people can help living things.
5. Make a cover for your book. Put the pages inside the cover.

elephant

ctories

Share what you learned.

1. What living things did you draw?
2. What does your book show about habitats?
3. How might the world look when you grow up?

A visit to a museum

You walk into the museum. A dinosaur skeleton is there. Wire holds the bones together. But who put the bones together?

Scientists sometimes find fossils of bones in rock. They send the rock to a museum. Then a **museum worker** digs the fossils out of the rock. Workers may use drills to dig out the fossils. At last, the fossils are out of the rock. Then museum workers put the skeleton together.

How does a drill work?

1 Air moves in and out through tubes.

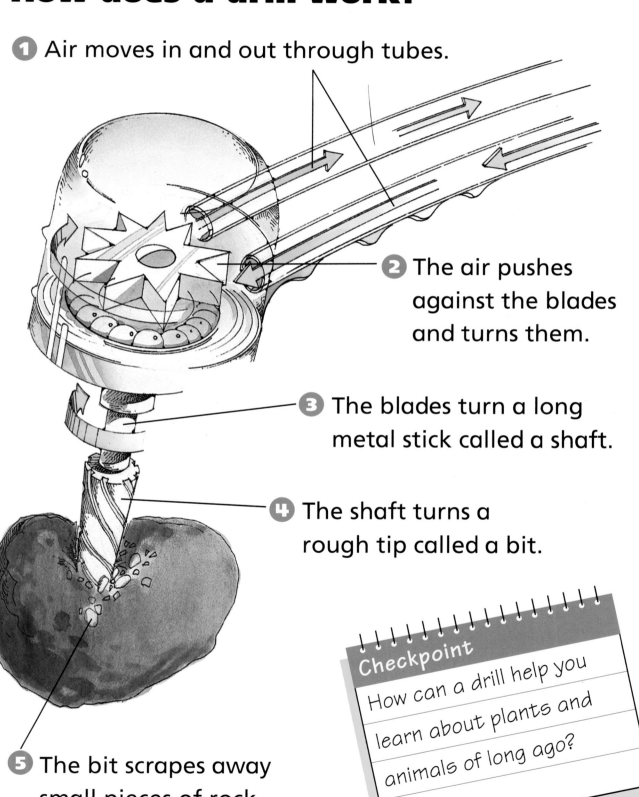

2 The air pushes against the blades and turns them.

3 The blades turn a long metal stick called a shaft.

4 The shaft turns a rough tip called a bit.

5 The bit scrapes away small pieces of rock.

Checkpoint

How can a drill help you learn about plants and animals of long ago?

Show what you know.

Where can you find fossils? Where can you learn about dinosaurs? You can go to a museum. A museum has objects that tell about life long ago. You can make a museum in your classroom. What can you put in your museum?

Plan a museum.

1. Pick a project you would like to do.
2. Find things you need to do your project.
3. Think about how to describe your project to someone else.

Make an exhibit.

Make your own fossil for the museum. Write a story about your fossil. Tell how your fossil formed. Display your fossil and the story.

Act out a story.

Act out a story about a dinosaur. Show how your dinosaur moved. Show other things about your dinosaur. How will you show why there are no more dinosaurs?

Tape-record a story.

Tape-record a story for the museum. Tell how living things can become endangered or extinct. Tell how people can help protect living things. Draw pictures for your story.

Share what you know.

1. Share your project about dinosaurs with your classmates.
2. What was fun about doing your project?

Making Things Move

Making Things Move

You can move your body in different ways. You can make objects move too. Sometimes moving things is not as easy as it looks. Can you make moving things easier?

Chapter 1

How Things Move

It might be easy for you to move a small toy. But you might need to use a strong force to move something heavy. Page **C 4**

Chapter 2
Magnets

How can one object push some things away and pull other things closer? Welcome to the amazing world of magnets! Page **C 22**

Chapter 3
Moving and Machines

You probably know how to use some kinds of machines. How do machines make moving things easier? Page **C 40**

In this module

People at Work   **C 60**
Module Review   **C 62**

At the end of the book

Kids Did It   6
Study Guide   18
Using Scientific Methods   26
Safety in Science   28
Experiment Skills   34
Glossary/Index   38

Chapter 1

How Things Move

Things are moving all around you. The leaves on a tree move. Clouds move across the sky. Cars, buses, and trains move on land. Airplanes move through the air.

Have you ever wondered what makes things move? Wind pushes these sailboats over the water. A person can use oars to pull the rowboat through the water. What makes the other boat move?

Discover Activity

How can you make a boat move?

1. Press some clay onto a block of wood.
2. Glue a square of paper on a craft stick to make a sail.
3. Stand the craft stick in the clay.
4. Float your boat in a large pan of water.
5. Try different ways to make your boat move.
6. **Tell about it.** Name two ways you can make your boat move.

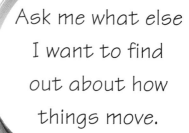

Ask me what else I want to find out about how things move.

What makes things move?

What did you do to make your boat move? You may have pulled it over the water with your fingers. Maybe you blew on the sail so that your breath pushed the boat. Your boat did not move by itself. You used a push or pull to make it move.

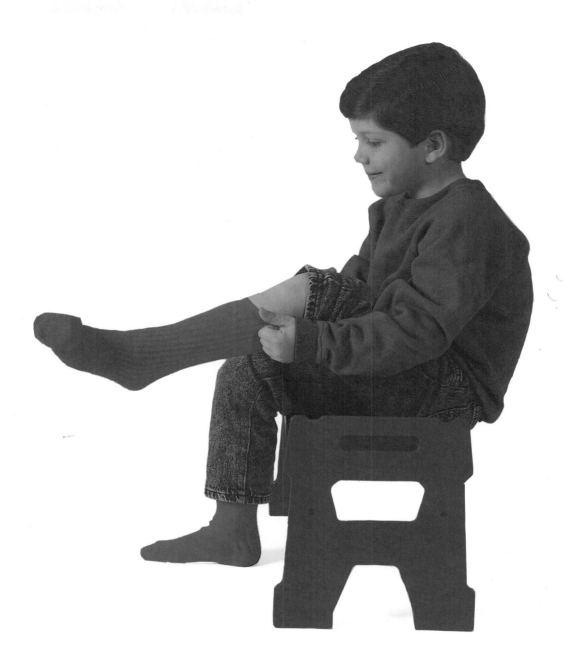

A push or pull that makes something move is a **force.** You might push a grocery cart. You might pull on your sock. What else can you push or pull?

Checkpoint

Draw something being moved by a force that pushes. Then draw something being moved by a force that pulls.

Where are the pushes and pulls?

Pretend you are at this playground. You can see pushes and pulls all around you. Find the girl playing in the sandbox. How is she using a push or pull?

How will the boys make the swings move? They could use a push or a pull to get them started. Find two other pushes and two other pulls.

Checkpoint

Tell about another push or pull you might see at a playground.

How can you move something farther?

Push a book across the floor. Use a weak push. How far does it move? What do you think will happen if you push the book using a strong push? Try it and see!

Does how hard you push the book change how far the book moves? You probably found the answer to that question. The book moves farther when you push it with a stronger force.

Push the can.

You will need: can masking tape

1. Kneel at one end of your classroom. Use a weak push to roll the can toward the other side of the room.
2. Roll the can different ways. Use weak and strong pushes.
3. Mark with tape the place where your can stops each time.

Checkpoint
Tell what you did to make the can move the farthest.

What do different forces do?

A push can be strong or weak. A pull can be strong or weak too. You can pull a swing. Will a strong pull or a weak pull make the swing move farther? How can you tell how strong a push or pull is?

Use different forces.

You will need: cover goggles metric ruler large rubber band pencil paper

1. Hold up the rubber band. Have your partner measure it.
2. Pull on the rubber band with a weak force. Have your partner measure how long the rubber band stretches.
3. Pull the rubber band with a stronger force. Have your partner measure it.
4. Draw three lines. Show how long the rubber band was when you used no force, a weak force, and a strong force.

Checkpoint
Tell what happens to the rubber band when the force gets stronger.

How does force move heavy things?

Pretend you are pulling a wagon. A friend jumps in. The wagon is harder to move! Will you need to use more force to pull it?

You will need:

 cover goggles

 large rubber band

 string

 3 small books

 metric ruler

Find out about it.

1 Tie one end of the string around a book. Tie the other end to the rubber band.

2 Have your partner measure the rubber band.

3 Pull on the rubber band until the book moves. Hold the book in place. Have your partner measure the rubber band.

4 Put two books on top of the first book. Pull on the rubber band until the books move.

5 Have your partner measure the rubber band.

Write about it.

Make a chart like this. Write how much the rubber band stretches to move the books.

number of books	length of rubber band
1 book	cm
3 books	cm

Checkpoint

1. Which number of books needed the most force to be moved?

2. Take Action! Find out what will happen if you add another book.

Where is it easier to pull things?

Suppose you want to move a big box full of toys. You pull the box across a rug. Then you pull the box across a bare floor. One way is easier because you use less force. Find out which way is easier.

Slide the book.

You will need:  string book rug

1. Tie one end of the string around the book.
2. Put the book on a rug. Pull the string until the book starts moving across the rug.
3. Put the book on a bare floor. Pull the string until the book moves across the floor.

Checkpoint

Tell if it is easier to move things across a rug or across a bare floor. Which time did you use less force?

What surfaces make moving things easier?

Wax paper and the top of a desk are smooth surfaces. Sandpaper and stones are rough surfaces. Is it easier to move an object across smooth surfaces or rough surfaces? You can find out. You can pull an object across each surface. You can measure how far a rubber band stretches when you pull.

1. Look at the chart. The rubber band stretched 1 cm when an object was pulled across wax paper. How far did the rubber band stretch when an object was pulled across stones?

surface	how far a rubber band stretched
sandpaper	7 cm
wax paper	1 cm
top of desk	2 cm
stones	6 cm

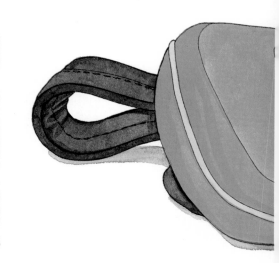

2. Make a chart like this one.

surface	how far the rubber band stretched						
sandpaper	▨	▨	▨	▨	▨	▨	▨
wax paper							
top of desk							
stones							

0   1   2   3   4   5   6   7

cm

3. The chart shows how much the rubber band stretched when sandpaper was used. Fill in the chart to show how much the rubber band stretched when other surfaces were used.

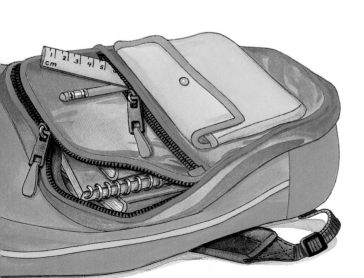

Checkpoint

1. Does the rubber band stretch more when smooth or rough surfaces are used?

2. Is it easier to move an object across smooth or rough surfaces?

What did you learn?

You found out that you need a push or a pull to make things move. Can you share what you know about forces? Make a poster that shows pushes and pulls.

You will need:  paper   magazines
scissors   glue   crayons

Make a poster.

1. Cut out pictures of objects that forces can move.
2. Find pictures of someone using a force that pushes an object. Glue the pictures on one part of the paper.
3. Find pictures of someone using a force that pulls an object. Glue the pictures on the other part of the paper.

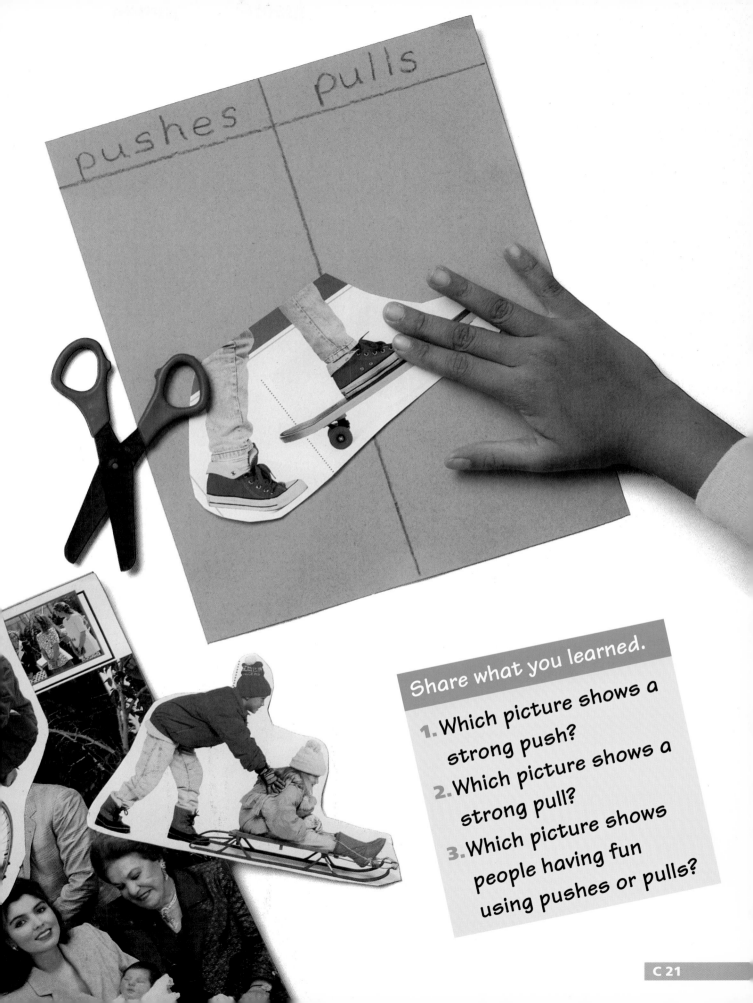

pushes   pulls

Share what you learned.

1. Which picture shows a strong push?
2. Which picture shows a strong pull?
3. Which picture shows people having fun using pushes or pulls?

C 21

Chapter 2
Magnets

Would you like to play with some of these magnets? You could have fun picking things up and moving things around.

But magnets are more than toys. They are important parts in radios, televisions, computers, and more! What else can magnets do? Let's find out!

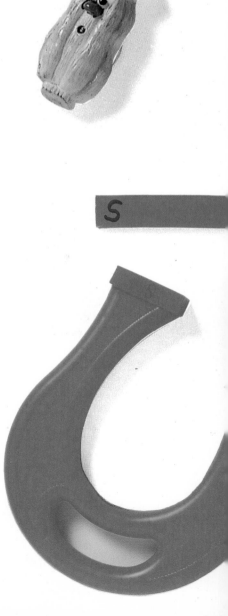

Discover Activity

What can magnets do to each other?

1. Put two magnets on a table. Slowly push the magnets toward each other. What happens?

2. Turn one magnet around.

3. Push the magnets toward each other again. What happens now?

4. **Tell about it.** Tell what happened when you pushed the magnets together.

Ask me what else I want to find out about magnets.

What are the poles of a magnet?

You saw one **magnet** move another magnet. Why do you think this happens? It happens because the ends of magnets are different from each other.

The two ends of magnets are called **poles**. Look at the poles of these magnets. The N stands for north pole. The S stands for south pole. A magnet pushes or pulls hardest at its poles. The N and the S show where the magnet is strongest.

If you put poles that are the same next to each other, they push apart. Two north poles next to each other would push apart. What would two south poles do?

Two poles that are not the same will pull together. A north and a south pole are not the same. If you put them next to each other, they pull together.

Checkpoint

Tell which places on a magnet push and pull hardest.

What can magnets do to other things?

You saw how magnets can pull together and push apart. Now find out what a magnet can do to other things.

You will need:

 strong magnet

 yarn

 markers

2 note cards

 20 small objects

Find out about it.

1. Make two circles of yarn on a table.

2. Write on note cards *pulls* and *does not pull.* Put a card in each circle.

3. Put the objects on the table.

4. Hold the magnet above each object.

5. Put objects the magnet pulls in the *pulls* circle. Put objects the magnet does not pull in the *does not pull* circle.

pulls

S

N

does not pull

Write about it.

Make a chart like this.
List the objects you placed
in each circle.

pulls	does not pull

Checkpoint

1. What kinds of things do magnets pull?

2. Take Action! Find three objects that can be pulled by a magnet.

How do you use magnets?

You probably use magnets in many ways. Some magnets can hold up important messages. Other magnets keep the doors of the refrigerator tightly closed. Magnets also keep the cabinet doors closed.

You can find magnets in many objects. Find objects in the picture that have magnets.

Checkpoint

Draw one way you use magnets.

magnet

magnets on bottom

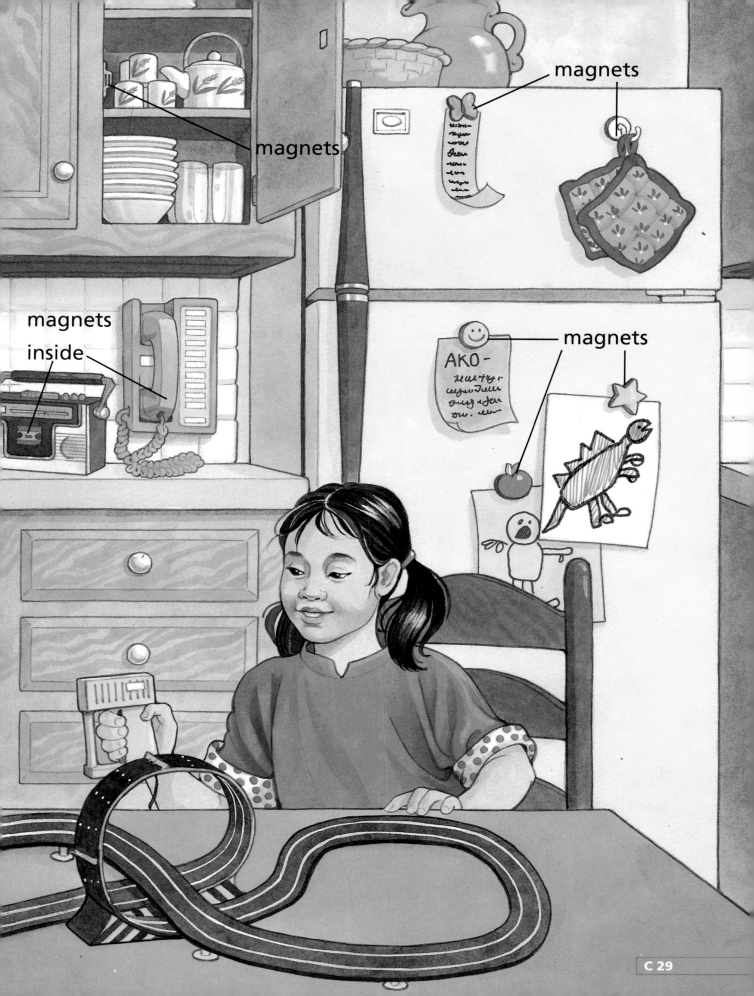

What can a magnet pull through?

How does a magnet hold up a note on a refrigerator? The sides of a refrigerator are metal. The magnet can pull through the note paper. Can a magnet pull through other things?

You will need:

 magnet

 paper clip

 paper

 cardboard

 plastic

 wood

 cloth

Find out about it.

1. Have your partner hold out a sheet of paper.

2. Hold a magnet on top of the paper. Hold a paper clip under the paper below the magnet.

3. Let go of the paper clip. What happens to it?

4. Do the same thing with cardboard, plastic, wood, and cloth. What happens?

Write about it. ✏️

Make a chart like this. Write what you learned.

	Can a magnet pull through these things?				
	paper	cardboard	plastic	wood	cloth
yes					
no					

Checkpoint

1. What can a magnet pull through?

2. **Take Action!** Find out if a magnet can pull through water.

Are all magnets strong?

Pretend you bring home two drawings you made in school. You hang one drawing on the refrigerator with a magnet. It stays up. Then you try to hang the other drawing. This time the drawing and the magnet fall to the floor! Could one magnet be stronger than the other? Do the activity to find out.

Find the strongest magnet.

You will need:  3 magnets  paper clips

1. Hold a magnet in your hand. Pick up a paper clip with the magnet.
2. Pick up another paper clip at the end of the first one.
3. Pick up more paper clips to make a chain. Pick up as many paper clips as you can.
4. Do the same thing with 2 other magnets.
5. Count the number of paper clips each magnet can hold.

Checkpoint

Draw a picture showing which magnet is strongest and which is weakest. Write down how you know.

How can you make a magnet?

How do you use batteries? You might use batteries to make a flashlight or radio work. Many toys run on batteries. Do you know that you can use a battery to make a magnet? Electricity from a battery can travel through a wire around a nail. Then the nail becomes a magnet.

Make a magnet.

You will need: cover goggles wire nail battery paper clip rubber band

1. Try to pick up the paper clip with the nail. Is the nail a magnet?
2. Wrap the wire around the nail 20 times.
3. Put the rubber band around the battery.
4. Put the ends of the wire on the battery.
5. Try to pick up the paper clip with the nail. What happens? Is the nail a magnet now?

Checkpoint
Tell what you did to change the nail into a magnet. Find out what else the nail can pick up.

How can you make a stronger magnet?

Suppose you wrap more wire around a nail. Would the nail become a stronger magnet? How can you tell which nail is the strongest magnet?

1. Look at the drawings of the nails. The wire is wrapped around nail A five times. How many times is the wire wrapped around nail B? How many times is the wire wrapped around nail C?

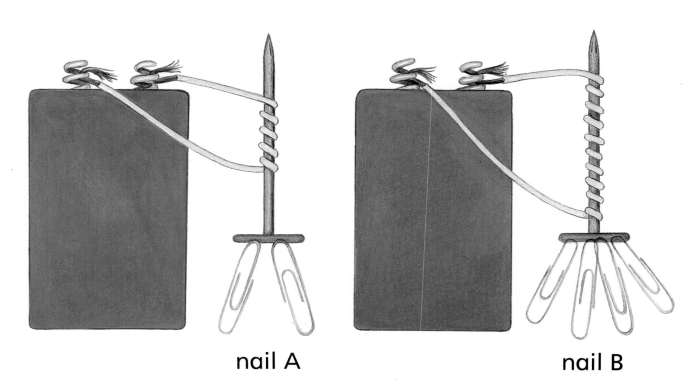

nail A   nail B

2. Draw a chart like this one.

	nail A	nail B	nail C
wire wrapped	5 times	10 times	8 times
paper clips			

3. Write down how many paper clips each nail picked up. Which nail picks up the most paper clips? Which nail has the wire wrapped around it the most times?

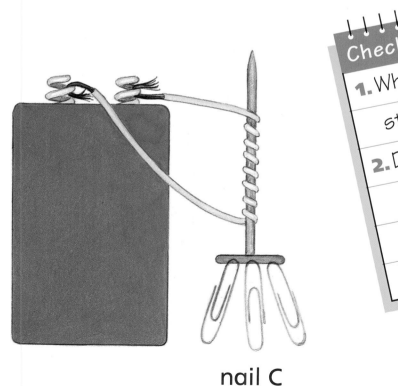

nail C

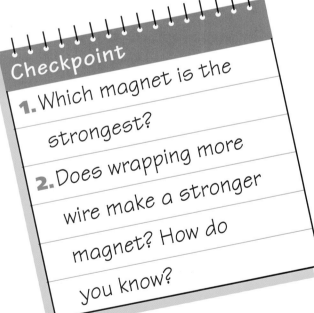

Checkpoint

1. Which magnet is the strongest?

2. Does wrapping more wire make a stronger magnet? How do you know?

What did you learn?

What do you know about magnets? You know that magnets have poles. They can pick up some metal things. Magnets can pull through things. You also know that some magnets are stronger than others. Now pretend that you sell magnets. Write an advertisement for magnets.

You will need:  paper pencil 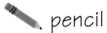 crayons

Write an ad for magnets.

1. Draw pictures for your ad.
2. You can show how a magnet can help clean your room. You can show how to make a game using magnets.
3. List ways a magnet can be useful.
4. Share your ad with your class.

MAGNET
MAGIC

1. How do the magnets in your ad help people?
2. Which way would you use magnets?

Chapter 3
Moving and Machines

Suppose you want to move the teddy bear. The picture shows a hard way to move it. Can you think of an easier way to move the bear?

You move things every day. Just look around you. Find things that you can move. What could help you make something easier to move?

What is the easiest way to move a box?

1. Drag the mystery box across the floor.

2. How hard did you work to drag that box?

3. Find things that can help you move the mystery box. Now how hard do you work?

4. **Tell about it.** Tell about things that helped you move the box.

Ask me what else I want to find out about how to move things.

What is a machine?

Close your eyes and think of a machine. Maybe you think of something big like a truck. Maybe you think of something small like a wagon. Anything that makes work easier is a **machine.** Bicycles and baby strollers are machines. Hammers are machines too. What other machines can you think of?

Remember how you moved the box in the last lesson. Maybe you used a machine! The girl in the picture put a skateboard under a box. The wheels can help move the box. A **wheel** is a kind of machine. How can you find out more about machines? You can try using them!

Checkpoint

Draw someone using a machine to make moving a heavy box easier.

How can a ramp help move things?

Pretend you are pushing a friend in a wheelchair. You come to the school. How will you get the heavy wheelchair to the school door? You see a **ramp.** The ramp can make your work easier.

A ramp is a kind of machine. A ramp helps you move things to a higher or lower place using less force. How can you use a ramp?

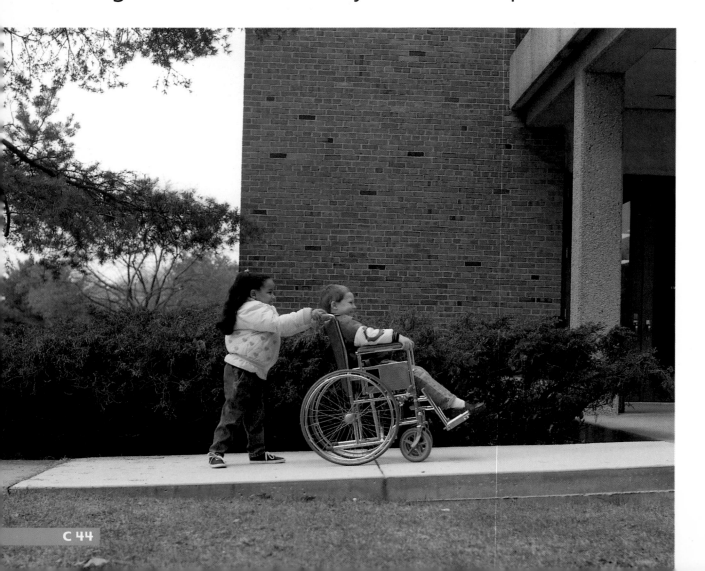

Use a ramp.

You will need: cover goggles rubber band

 book string chair  ramp

1. Tie the string around the book. Tie the rubber band to the string.
2. Put the book on the floor next to the chair.
3. Pull on the rubber band to raise the book as high as the chair seat.
4. Lean a ramp against the chair. Put the book at the bottom of the ramp.
5. Hold the rubber band. Pull the book up the ramp as high as the chair seat. How does the ramp help you move the book?

Checkpoint

Draw the easiest way to move the book. Tell how you know.

How can a lever help move things?

The children in the picture are playing on a seesaw. They can lift each other into the air. A seesaw is another kind of machine. It is called a **lever.** A lever helps you move things using less force. You can push down on one end of a lever to lift something on the other end.

Use a lever.

You will need: 📕 book   ✏️ 3 pencils
📏 metric ruler   🧻 masking tape

1. Put the pencils under the ruler.
2. Put the book on one end of the ruler.
3. Push down the other end of the ruler. How hard do you push to move the book?
4. Move the pencils closer to the book. Push down again.
5. Move the pencils farther away from the book. Push down again. How hard did you push down this time?

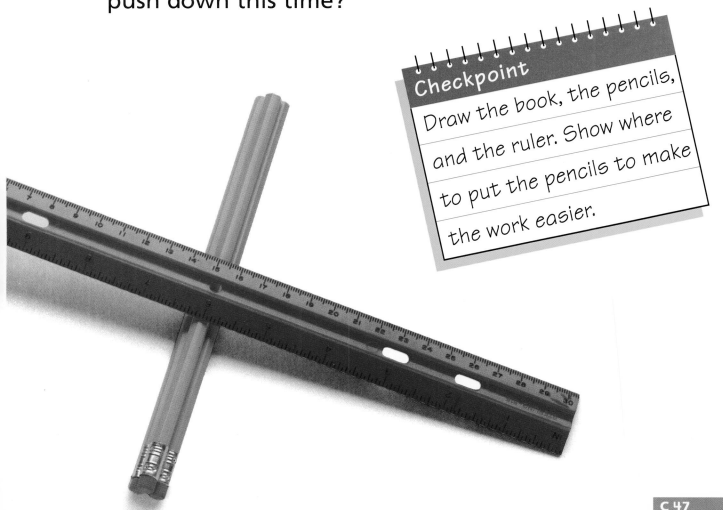

Checkpoint

Draw the book, the pencils, and the ruler. Show where to put the pencils to make the work easier.

How do ball bearings help move things?

Ball bearings are smooth round balls that can help move things. You can find out how ball bearings work.

You will need:

 cover goggles

 large book

 10 to 15 marbles

 jar lid with rim

 string

 large rubber band

Find out about it.

1 Tie the string around the book. Tie the string to the rubber band.

2 Place the book on the jar lid.

3 Pull on the rubber band until the book starts moving. Notice how much the rubber band stretches.

4 Put the marbles under the jar lid. Put the book on the lid.

5 Pull on the rubber band until the book moves. Notice how much the rubber band stretches.

Write about it. ✏️

Make a chart like this. Draw how the rubber band looks when the book moves.

book	how the rubber band looks
without marbles	
with marbles	

Checkpoint

1. Did the marbles help move the book? How do you know?

2. Take Action! Draw an imaginary toy that has ball bearings.

How are body parts like a machine?

Mmm! The milk tastes so good. You lift the glass for another sip. Your arm is working like a machine. Your arm is a lever when you bend it to lift the glass.

Other parts of your body can work like machines too. What happens when you throw a ball into the air? Your whole arm moves around in your shoulder. The upper end of your arm bone moves like a ball bearing.

Checkpoint

Write about one part of your body that works like a machine.

How do you move?

Muscles and **bones** help you move. Bones move when muscles pull on them.

Find the place where the leg bones come together at the knee. A place where bones come together is a **joint.** Joints help your body bend, turn, and twist.

Now find the muscles near the joint. These muscles work with the bones to help move the girl's leg.

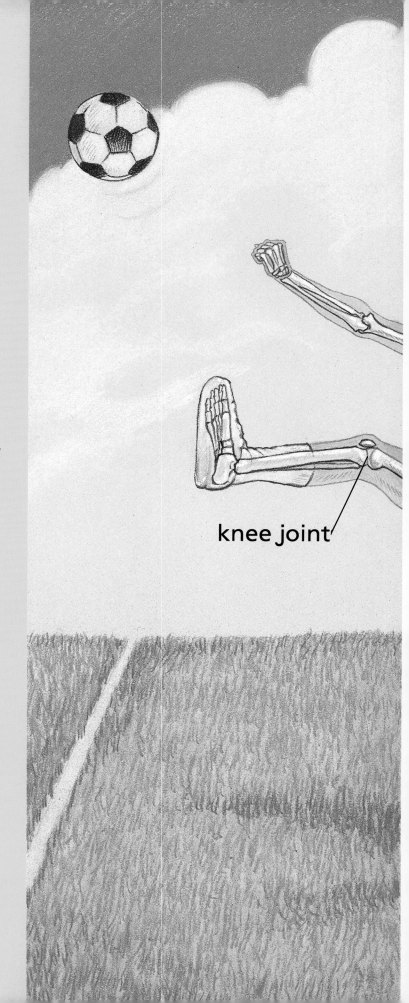

knee joint

Checkpoint
Feel the bones and muscles that move your own leg.

Bones

Muscles

How do muscles work?

How do bones and muscles work together? You can do this activity to find out how they work.

You will need:

 cover goggles

 2 cardboard bones

 long balloon

 paper fastener

Find out about it.

1 Get cardboard models of bones from your teacher.

2 Put the bones together with the paper fastener.

3 Blow air into the balloon. Tie a knot in each end of the balloon.

4 Slide the knots of the balloon muscle into the slits in the cardboard bones.

5 Move the bones. How does the muscle look?

Write about it. ✏️

Make a chart like this one. Write what you found out.

bones	How does the muscle look?
bones open wide	
bones close together	

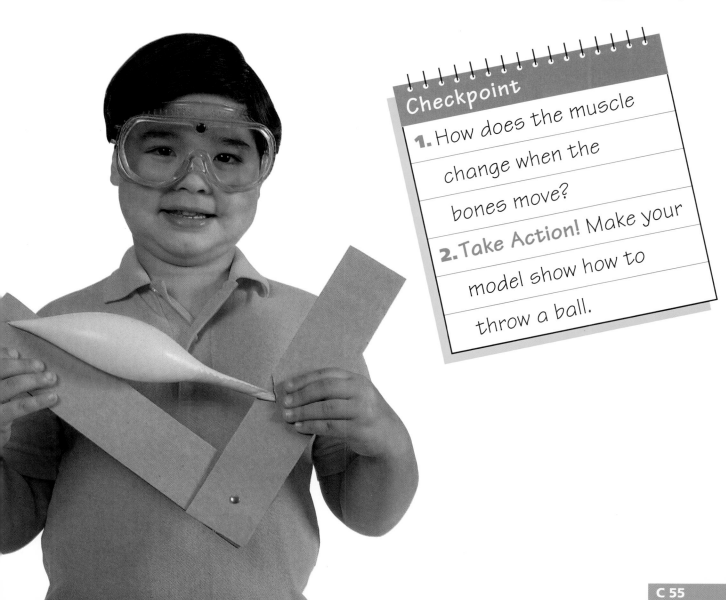

Checkpoint

1. How does the muscle change when the bones move?

2. Take Action! Make your model show how to throw a ball.

How many bones do body parts have?

Think about the bones in your body. Some body parts have more bones than other body parts. You can find out how many bones some body parts have.

1. Look at the picture. The hand has 27 bones. How many bones are in your foot?
2. Copy the chart below.
3. Write how many bones are in different parts of your body.

part of body	number of bones
head	22
arm	
hand	
leg	
foot	
spine	

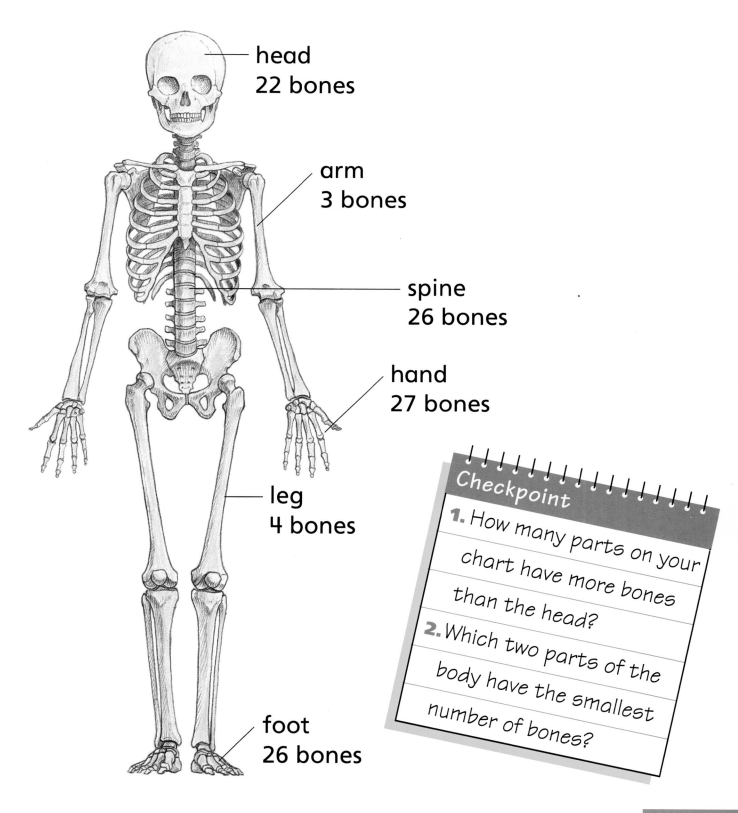

head
22 bones

arm
3 bones

spine
26 bones

hand
27 bones

leg
4 bones

foot
26 bones

Checkpoint

1. How many parts on your chart have more bones than the head?

2. Which two parts of the body have the smallest number of bones?

What did you learn?

You learned about some machines that help move things. You know about ramps and levers and ball bearings. You learned that some parts of your body act like machines! Now you can make your own book about machines.

Make a book.

You will need: 2 sheets of paper   pencil   crayons   construction paper

1. Draw a picture that shows you moving something with a machine.
2. Write the name of the machine at the top of the picture.
3. Draw a picture that shows you using a body part like a machine.
4. Write a sentence that tells how the body part is like a machine.
5. Make a cover for your book. Put the pages inside the cover.

My arm is

Share what you learned.

1. How do the machines in your book help you?
2. What machines would you use to move books from one room to another?

A visit to a bicycle factory

A bicycle factory is a busy place. You hear noisy machines. You see many workers. You might wonder what these workers do.

It takes many **factory workers** to make a bicycle. Each worker needs to know how to use special machines. Some workers make bicycle parts. Some workers spray the bicycles with paint. Other workers put the bicycle parts together. One day you might see the bicycles in a store!

How does a bicycle work?

1 The frame of the bicycle holds other parts of the bicycle together.

5 The brakes make the bicycle stop. Some bicycles have levers that work the brakes.

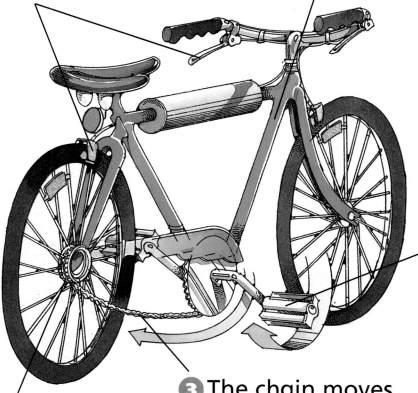

2 The pedals move the chain.

3 The chain moves the back wheel.

4 The ball bearings help the wheels move around.

Checkpoint
How does a bicycle make it easier for you to get from one place to another?

Show what you know.

Think about things you see in a playground. Some things can move up and down. Some things can move around. Now think about how you could plan a new playground. Use what you know about force, magnets, and machines to help you.

Plan your playground.

1. Choose a project to do.
2. What will you do first?
3. What will your project look like when it is finished?
4. Decide how to share your project.

Make a chart.

Imagine making rides in a playground go faster or slower. Imagine making rides go higher or lower. Make a chart of playground rides. Show ways you can change how the rides move.

ride   change   what happens

Invent a ride.

Use what you know about forces, magnets, and machines to invent a playground ride. Build a model that works. Tell what makes your ride move.

Draw a picture.

Draw a picture of a playground. Show children pushing and pulling things. Tell how your body works as a machine when you play.

Share what you know.

1. Share your project.
2. How do the other projects tell about moving things?
3. What do you like best about your project?

The Earth and Sky

The Earth and Sky

Close your eyes and imagine the sky. You might think of the sun, or the moon, or the stars. Look where you are standing. What can you learn about the earth?

Chapter 1

The Sun

When you think about the sun, you might think of a big yellow ball. But what is the sun really like? Page **D 4**

Chapter 2

The Moon and Stars

The moon and stars light up the night sky. What makes the moon and stars shine so brightly? Page **D 24**

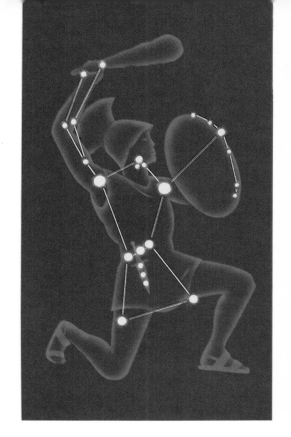

Chapter 3

Looking at the Earth

The earth looks different in different places. But no matter where on the earth you are, you can see land or water. Page **D 42**

In this module
People at Work	**D 60**
Module Review	**D 62**

At the end of the book
Kids Did It	8
Study Guide	22
Using Scientific Methods	26
Safety in Science	28
Experiment Skills	36
Glossary/Index	38

Chapter 1
The Sun

Think about day and night. How are they different? Why is it light during the day? Why is it dark at night?

You know that the sky looks different during the day and at night. You see the sun in the sky during the day. Can you see the sun at night?

How are day and night different?

1 Pretend a flashlight is the sun. Pretend a ball is the earth.

2 Mark a spot on the ball with a piece of tape.

3 Hold the flashlight still.

4 Move the ball so it is day at the piece of tape.

5 Move the ball so it is night at the piece of tape.

6 **Tell about it.** Tell how you moved the ball to make night and day.

Ask me what else I want to find out about the sun.

How does day turn into night?

Day and night happen because the earth turns. Then the sun lights different parts of the earth.

Look at the top pictures. Find San Francisco on the part of the earth where the sun is shining. The city has day. Look at the bottom pictures. The earth has turned. The sun is not shining on San Francisco. Is it day or night there?

Checkpoint

Write a story about how day and night happen.

Sun

Earth

X

San Francisco

Sun

Earth

X

San Francisco

How big is the sun?

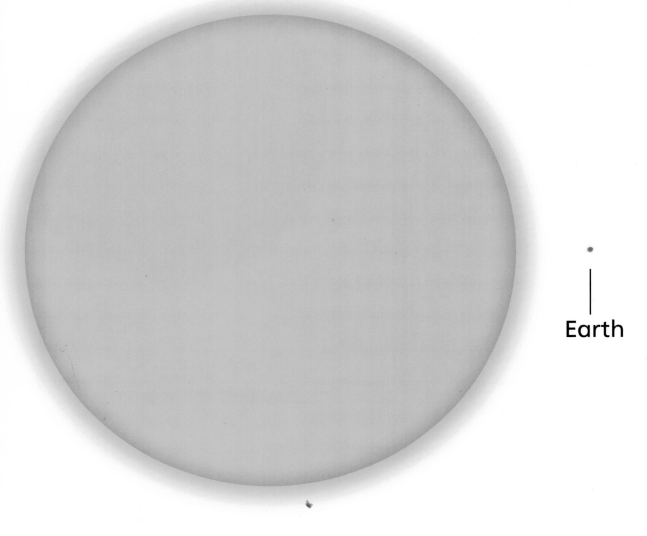

Earth

Sun

How big do you think the sun is? Is it larger or smaller than the earth? Look at the drawing to find out.

You can see that the sun is much larger than the earth. Let's find out why the sun might look small in the sky.

Show why the sun looks small.

You will need: metric ruler paper plate

1. Hold up the plate. Have your partner measure across the plate.
2. Move back six steps. Your partner should not move.
3. Have your partner measure how big the plate looks again. Do this by holding the ruler in front of the plate.
4. What happens to the size of the plate?

Checkpoint
Tell how you made the plate look smaller.

What is the sun?

You learned that the sun is big. Now let's find out some other things about the sun. The sun is our closest star. You can see that it is shaped like a ball. The sun is made of very hot gases.

What do you think the sun does for the earth? The sun gives the earth light. Sunlight makes daytime on the earth. Sunlight warms the earth too.

Show that sunlight warms the earth.

You will need: 2 plates timer

 2 ice cubes

1. Put an ice cube on each plate.
2. Put one plate in a place that gets sunlight. Put the other plate in a place that gets no sunlight.
3. Time how long each ice cube takes to melt.

Checkpoint

Draw a picture of an ice cube in a place where it melts fast.

How does sunlight help plants grow?

Think about a park. What plants might grow there? Is the sun important to plants? You can find out if plants need sunlight to grow.

You will need:

 2 plants

 water

Find out about it.

1 Put one plant in a sunny place.

2 Put the other plant in a dark place.

3 Water each plant.

4 Look at both plants each day.

Write about it.

Make a chart like this one. Write down what you see each day.

days	plant in sunny place	plant in dark place
day 1		
day 2		
day 3		
day 4		
day 5		

Checkpoint

1. What happens to each plant?
2. **Take Action!** Draw a picture of each plant on day 1. Draw a picture of each plant on day 5.

How does the sun help animals?

You already learned how the sun is important to plants. But how does the sun help animals?

Animals need food to stay alive. Where do animals get food? Some animals use plants for food. Some animals eat other living things that use plants for food. The plants need sunlight to grow.

The sun is important to animals in another way too. Can you guess how? You already know that sunlight warms the earth. Sunlight also helps animals stay warm.

Checkpoint

Paint a picture showing how the sun is important to animals.

How can you use sunlight?

Pretend you are playing in the sun. Does your skin feel warm? Think of other things that might feel warm in the sun.

Did you know that the sun can cook food? When you use the sun to cook, you use **solar energy**. Solar energy is energy that comes from the sun. You can try using the sun to cook some food.

Make a solar oven.

You will need: foil cardboard box

 tape small potato plastic wrap

1. Tape the foil to the inside of the box. Be sure the foil is shiny side up.
2. Put the potato in the box.
3. Cover the box with plastic wrap.
4. Put the box in the sun.
5. Cook the potato.

Checkpoint

Draw a magazine ad for a solar oven. Tell how it can cook food.

How do coal and oil come from sunlight?

You used solar energy from the sun. People also use **fuels** such as coal and oil for energy. People can burn these fuels to get heat they can use. The sun helped make coal and oil.

Long ago the earth looked like this picture. The sun helped these plants grow. Animals used the plants as food. When the plants and animals died, sand and soil covered them. Over many years the plants and animals changed into oil and coal.

Checkpoint

Do a radio commercial for coal or oil. Tell how the fuels formed. Tell how they can help people.

How fast can you cook food in a solar oven?

Remember how you cooked food in a solar oven? You found out how long a potato takes to cook. Do you think all foods take the same time to cook? Let's find out.

cooking time		
1 to 2 hours	3 to 4 hours	5 to 8 hours
fruit	vegetables	soup
egg	bread	stew
fish	most meat	

1. Look at the chart. Bread and vegetables take 3 to 4 hours to cook. Name the foods that take the most time to cook.

2. Draw a chart like this one.

foods	cooking time		
	1–2 hours	3–4 hours	5–8 hours
egg	▨▨▨▨		
most meat		▨▨▨▨	
fish			
vegetables			
stew			
bread			
fruit			
soup			

3. The chart shows how long it takes to cook an egg and most meat. Color your chart to show how long the other foods take to cook.

Checkpoint

1. Does fish or bread take longer to cook?

2. What foods would be best to cook if you were in a hurry?

What did you learn?

You know that the sun gives light and warmth to the earth. You also know that all living things need the sun. Now draw a cartoon strip to show the things you learned.

You will need: pencil   crayons

paper   tape   markers

Make a cartoon strip.

1. Think about why the sun is important.
2. Tape pieces of paper together to make a long strip.
3. Draw lines across the strip to make squares.
4. Write the name of your cartoon strip in the first square.
5. Draw pictures in the other squares. Show different ways the sun is important.
6. Share your cartoon strip with a classmate.

Share what you learned.

1. What is your favorite part of your cartoon strip? Tell why.
2. What fun things can you do because of the sun?

Chapter 2
The Moon and Stars

"Star light, star bright. First star I see tonight." Maybe you will say this when you look up at the sky tonight!

What things do you see in the night sky? What do you know about these things? What do you wonder about?

What does the night sky look like?

1. Draw a picture of things you might see in the sky at night.
2. Write a sentence that tells about the night sky.
3. **Tell about it.** Tell about the things you drew in the night sky.

Ask me what else I want to find out about the night sky.

How are other stars like the sun?

Did you draw stars in your picture of the night sky? Sometimes you can see many stars on a clear night.

Remember that the sun is a **star.** Like the sun, all stars are made up of hot gases. Stars shine because the gases glow. You can see the light from the glowing, hot gases.

You know that the sun looks smaller than it really is. It looks small because it is far away. Other stars look small because they are far away too. These stars look smaller than the sun. They are even farther away from the earth than the sun is. Many of these stars are really much bigger than the sun.

Checkpoint

List ways the sun and other stars are alike.

How are stars grouped?

Long ago, people imagined that lines connected the stars. The lines and stars looked like pictures in the sky. People made up stories about the pictures.

Count the stars that make up the hunter's belt. Find the stars that make pictures of the lion and the bear. Now look at the last box. Use your finger to connect some stars to make a picture.

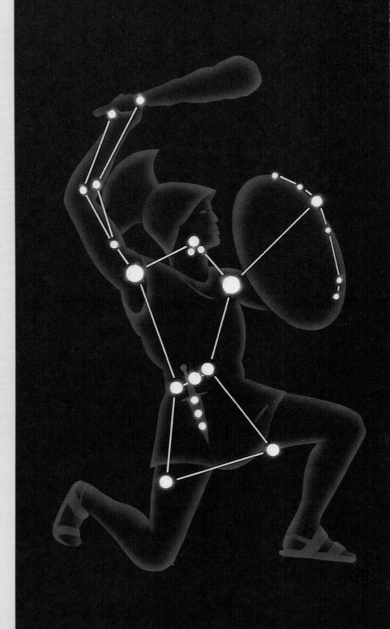

Orion the Hunter

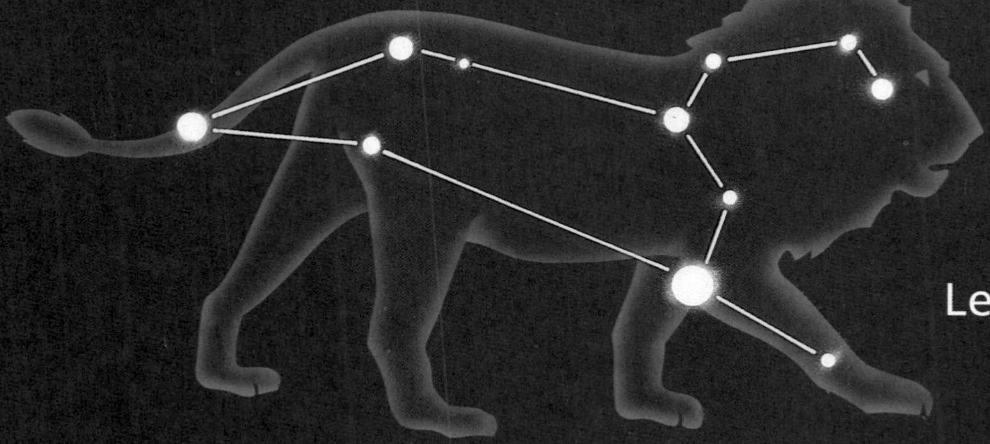

Leo the Lion

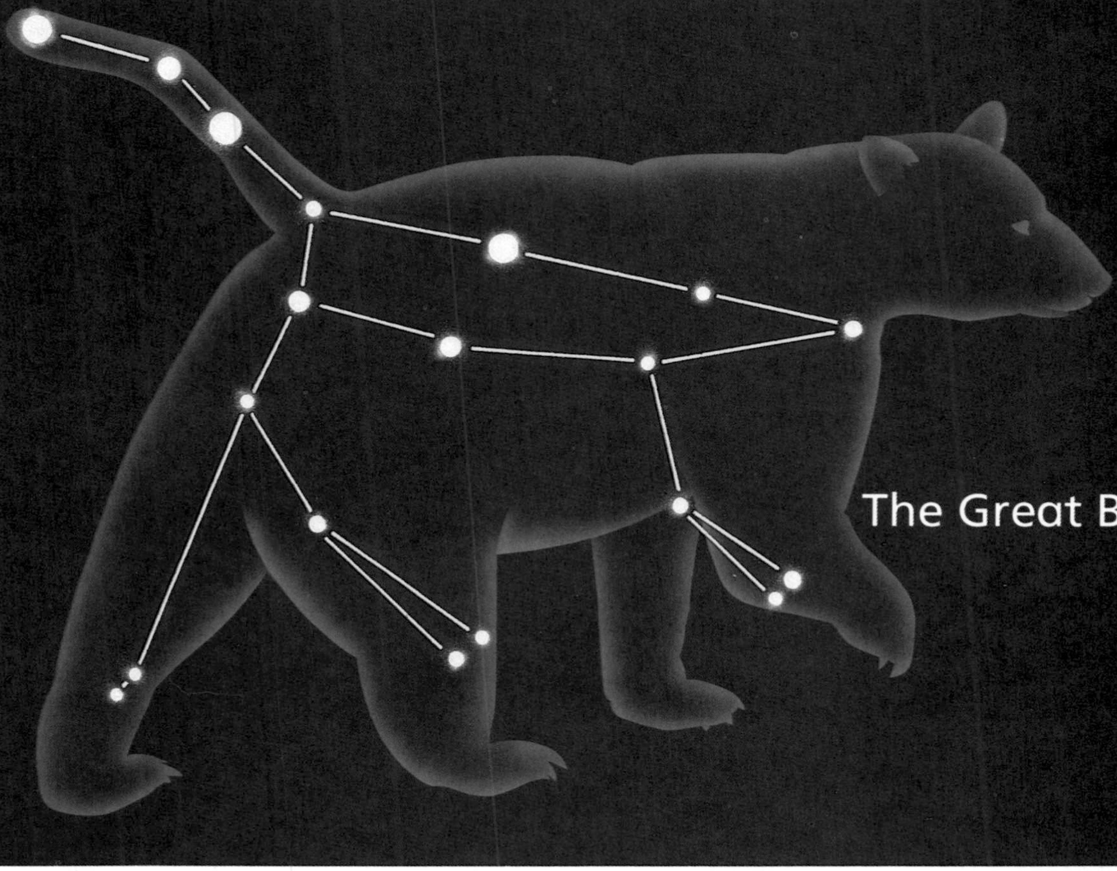

The Great Bear

Cassiopeia

What star group can you make?

A group of stars that forms a picture in the sky is a **constellation**. Some constellations have shapes that look like animals or people. You can make your own constellation.

You will need:

 cover goggles

 black construction paper

 pencil

 flashlight

Find out about it.

1 Poke holes through the paper with a pencil. Do not tear the paper.

2 Make the room dark. Hold the paper up facing the wall.

3 Shine a flashlight so the light comes through the holes. What picture do you see on the wall?

Write about it. ✏️

Make a chart like this one. Draw stars.
Connect the stars to make a constellation.

my stars	my constellation

Checkpoint

1. How many stars are in your constellation?

2. Take Action! Pretend you are a teacher. Tell your class about your constellation.

What else is in the night sky?

You can see many stars in the night sky. What else can you see? You often can see the **moon** shine in the night sky.

The moon is the brightest thing in the night sky. But the moon is not a star. Where does the moon's light come from?

Moonlight comes from the sun. Sunlight shining on the moon makes the moon shine. You can show how the sun makes the moon shine.

Light up the moon.

You will need: small ball flashlight globe

1. Make the room dark.
2. Pretend the ball is the moon. Pretend the flashlight is the sun.
3. Hold the ball in one hand. Hold the globe in the other hand.
4. Have your partner shine the flashlight on the ball and globe.

Checkpoint

Tell what makes the moon shine.

What does the moon look like?

What would you find if you could visit the moon? The moon has no water, air, or living things. It does have rocks, soil, and mountains. The moon also has many holes called **craters.**

Long ago, rocks from space crashed into the moon. The rocks made craters. Some craters are small. Other craters are very big. You can find out why craters are different sizes.

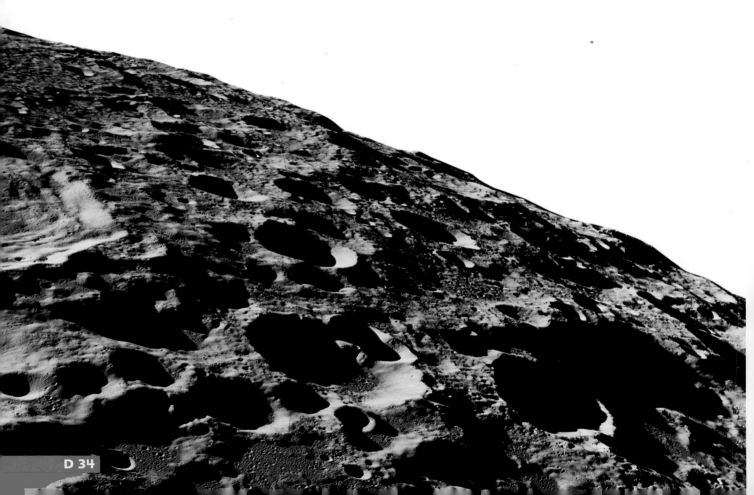

Make craters.

You will need: pan of sand marble golf ball

1. Hold the marble as high as your waist. Drop it into the sand.
2. Pick up the marble. Observe how big the hole in the sand is.
3. Hold the golf ball as high as your waist. Drop it into a different part of the sand.
4. Pick up the ball. Observe how big the hole in the sand is.

Checkpoint

Tell what makes the bigger crater. What makes craters different sizes?

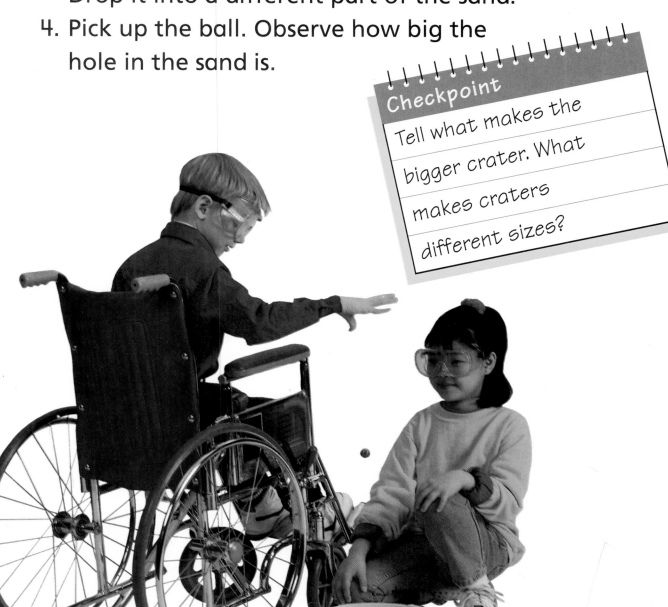

What shapes does the moon have?

Some nights the moon looks like a whole circle in the sky. Other nights the moon looks like part of a circle. But the moon is always the same shape. One side of the moon is always lit. Why does the shape of the moon seem to change?

The moon moves around the earth. You only see the part of the moon that has light shining on it. Sometimes you see all of the lighted side. Sometimes you see part of the lighted side. So you see different shapes of the moon.

The shapes of the moon are called **phases.** The pictures show four phases of the moon. Point to the phases you have seen.

Checkpoint

Draw pictures of two phases of the moon. Use crayons to color your pictures.

How does the shape of the moon change?

Each day the moon seems to change shape. It moves all the way around the earth in about a month. The moon goes through all its phases in about a month.

1. Look at the calendar. It shows what the moon looked like on each day of a month. On June 15 you could see a full moon. What could you see on June 7?

2. Make a chart like this one.

3. Use the calendar to fill in the chart. Write down the dates you would see each of the phases of the moon.

phase of moon		date
full moon		
half moon		
crescent moon		

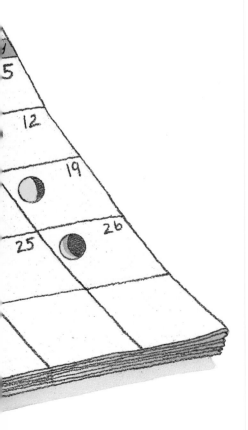

Checkpoint

1. What two days had crescent moons?

2. About how many days does the moon take to go from a full moon to a half moon?

What did you learn?

Now you know some things about the night sky. You know what the words *constellation* and *phase* mean. Play a game to show what else you learned.

You will need: ☐ 10 note cards ✏️ pencil

Play a memory game.

1. Think of five words that tell about the night sky. Write each word on two cards.
2. Mix up your cards.
3. Place the cards facedown on the table. Decide who will play first.
4. Turn over two cards. Read the words. Then use each word in a sentence.
5. If the words match, keep the cards. Turn the cards down if the words do not match.
6. Take turns until all the cards are matched.
7. Play the game again. Use the cards your partner made.

Chapter 3
Looking at the Earth

You are digging a hole in the ground. You want to find out what makes up the earth. You might dig through sand, soil, or clay. What else can you find when you dig? Let's find out what the earth is made of!

What parts of the earth can you find?

1 Look at the ground near school. Find nonliving things that make up the earth.

2 Put the things in plastic **bags**.

3 Write the name of each thing on tape. Put the tape on the bag.

4 Share what you found with your classmates.

5 **Tell about it.** Tell what kinds of things everyone found.

Ask me what else I want to find out about the earth.

What makes up the earth?

What did you find that makes up the earth? You might find mostly rocks, soil, and water. Look closely at what you found. Is all the soil alike? Is all the water alike? Are all the rocks alike?

You probably found many different kinds of rocks. Look at all the rocks your class found. How could you sort the rocks?

Sort the rocks.

You will need: rocks

1. Work with a group. Put all the rocks the group found in a pile.
2. Look at the rocks carefully. Look at their size and color.
3. Touch the rocks. Do they all feel the same?
4. Sort the rocks different ways. Group them by how they are alike.

Checkpoint

Tell how you sorted the rocks.

What is soil like?

You looked closely at rocks. Now look closely at soil. Soil has bits of rock in it. What else do you think is in soil?

You will need:

 cover goggles

 soil

 toothpicks

 hand lens

 white paper

 spoon

 paper towels

 cup of water

Find out about it.

1 Put soil on the white paper.

2 Move the soil with a toothpick.

3 Look at the soil with a hand lens. List the things you find.

4 Drop 2 spoonfuls of soil into the water. Look for bubbles of air.

5 Put a spoonful of soil between 2 paper towels.

6 Press the towels together. Look for wet spots on the towels. Where did the wetness come from?

Write about it.

Make a chart like this one. Write down or draw the things you found in the soil.

things in soil

Checkpoint

1. What nonliving things did you find in soil?

2. Take Action! Draw a picture that shows how you can sort the things you found.

What are different kinds of land?

You might have seen pictures of land in different places. Land in some places is flat. Land in other places has hills. Some places have mountains and valleys. What is the land like where you live?

You can make a model of what the land looks like. You can make a model of your favorite place. You can make a model of the land where you live. Here's how!

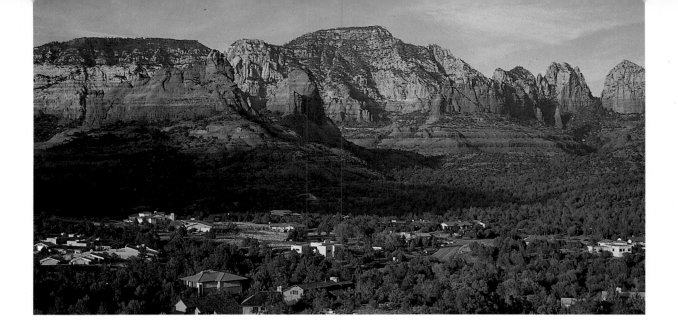

Make a model of land.

You will need: aluminum foil cardboard

 modeling clay sand rocks

 small pebbles

1. Cover the cardboard with clay. Use brown clay for soil. Use green clay for grass.
2. Use clay to shape hills, mountains, and other kinds of land. Put them on the cardboard.
3. Cover the clay with sand to show beaches and deserts. Use pebbles or rocks to make rocky places.
4. Use aluminum foil for water.

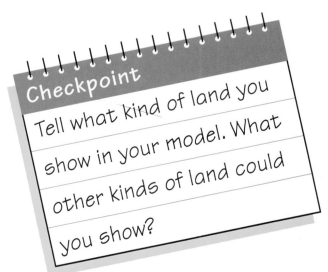

Checkpoint

Tell what kind of land you show in your model. What other kinds of land could you show?

Where is water on the earth?

Where do you see water on the earth? You might see water in puddles after the rain. You might see water in pools or ponds. You can see water in these pictures.

Most of the water on the earth is in oceans. Water is also in lakes, rivers, and streams. There are even rivers under the ground.

Checkpoint

Draw the places where you could find water.

ocean

stream

river

lake

How are salt water and fresh water different?

You know that most of the water on earth is in oceans. Do you know that ocean water is salty? You cannot drink the salty water in oceans.

The water you drink every day is fresh water. It does not taste salty. You find fresh water in most rivers, lakes, and streams. Let's find out how fresh water and salt water are different.

Find out about salt water and fresh water.

You will need: 2 plastic cups   water   spoon   salt   masking tape   piece of soap   marker

1. Write the words *fresh water* on a piece of tape. Write the words *salt water* on tape.
2. Put 1 tape on each cup.
3. Fill each cup half way with water.
4. Add 4 spoonfuls of salt to the *salt water* cup.
5. Observe the water in each cup. How does the water look and smell?
6. Put a piece of soap in each cup. Watch what happens.

Checkpoint

List two ways salt water and fresh water are different.

What is around the earth?

Air is all around the earth. You found air in the soil. Air is around and inside you. You cannot see air, but you can see what it does. You can feel air when it moves.

Moving air is wind. Wind makes trees bend and kites fly. It helps push sailboats across water. What else does wind do?

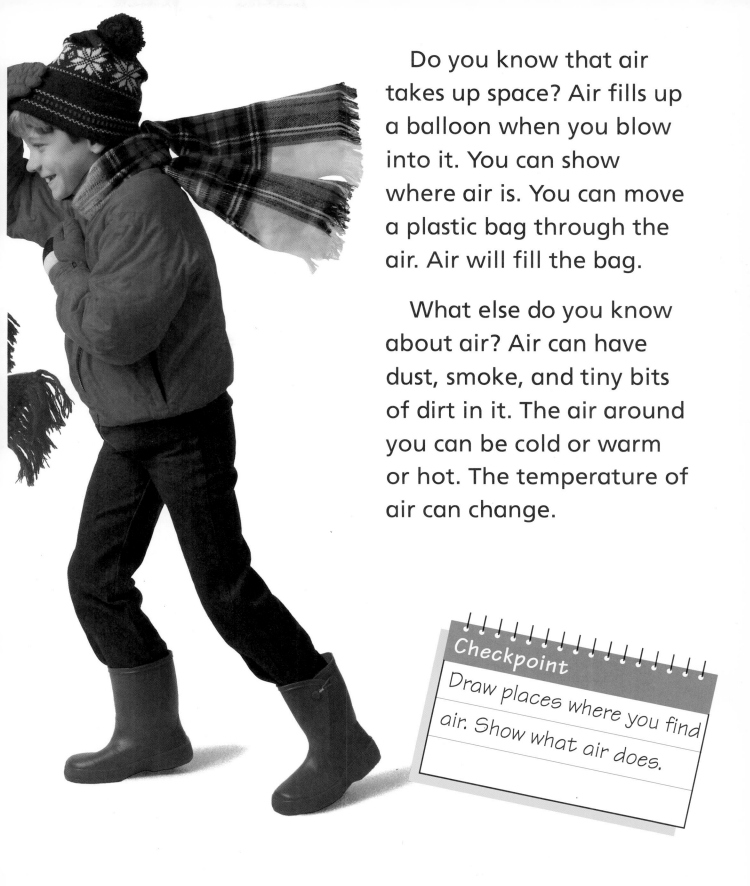

Do you know that air takes up space? Air fills up a balloon when you blow into it. You can show where air is. You can move a plastic bag through the air. Air will fill the bag.

What else do you know about air? Air can have dust, smoke, and tiny bits of dirt in it. The air around you can be cold or warm or hot. The temperature of air can change.

Checkpoint

Draw places where you find air. Show what air does.

Does the sun heat things the same way?

You know a lot about the earth and the air around the earth. Remember that the earth is heated by the sun. Let's find out if the sun heats air, soil, and water in the same way.

1. Look at the air, water, and soil. They were all the same temperature. Then they were put in the sun for 30 minutes.

2. Read the temperature on each thermometer. What is the temperature of the soil?

3. Make a chart like this one.

4. Fill in the rest of the chart.

time	soil temperature	water temperature	air temperature
at start	25°	25°	25°
after 30 minutes			

Checkpoint

1. Where did you see the highest temperature after 30 minutes?

2. Does air, soil, or water heat up the most?

What did you learn?

You learned about rocks, soil, and water. You learned how land looks in different places. You also learned that air is all around the earth. Now you can make a poster to show about the earth.

You will need: 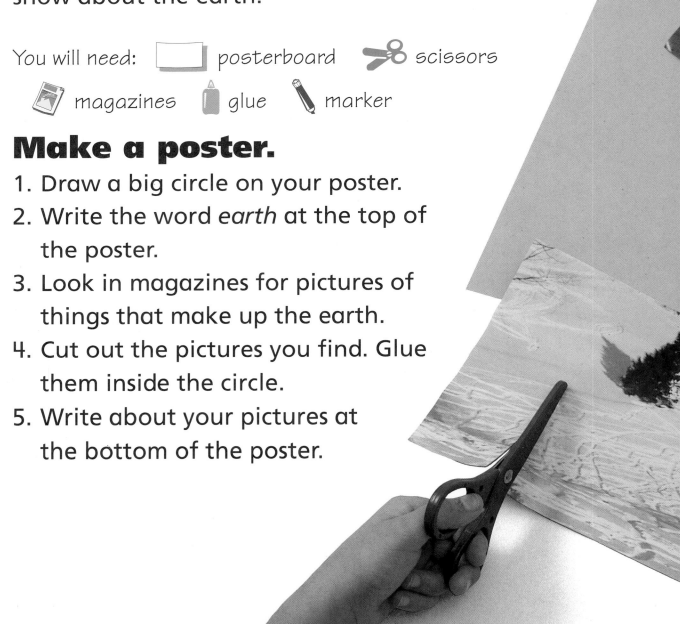 posterboard ✂ scissors
📖 magazines 🧴 glue ✏ marker

Make a poster.

1. Draw a big circle on your poster.
2. Write the word *earth* at the top of the poster.
3. Look in magazines for pictures of things that make up the earth.
4. Cut out the pictures you find. Glue them inside the circle.
5. Write about your pictures at the bottom of the poster.

earth

Share what you learned.

1. What pictures look like the part of the earth where you live?
2. What picture of the earth do you like the best? Tell why.

A visit to a planetarium

At the planetarium you sit in a round dark room. You look up. What you see looks like the sky! You can see how the sun lights the moon. You can see different shapes of the moon. You can even see stars.

A person who studies the stars and planets is an **astronomer.** Stars and planets give off light. Telescopes help astronomers see the light from stars and planets.

How does a telescope work?

1 Light goes into the telescope.

4 The lens in the eyepiece makes stars and planets look bigger.

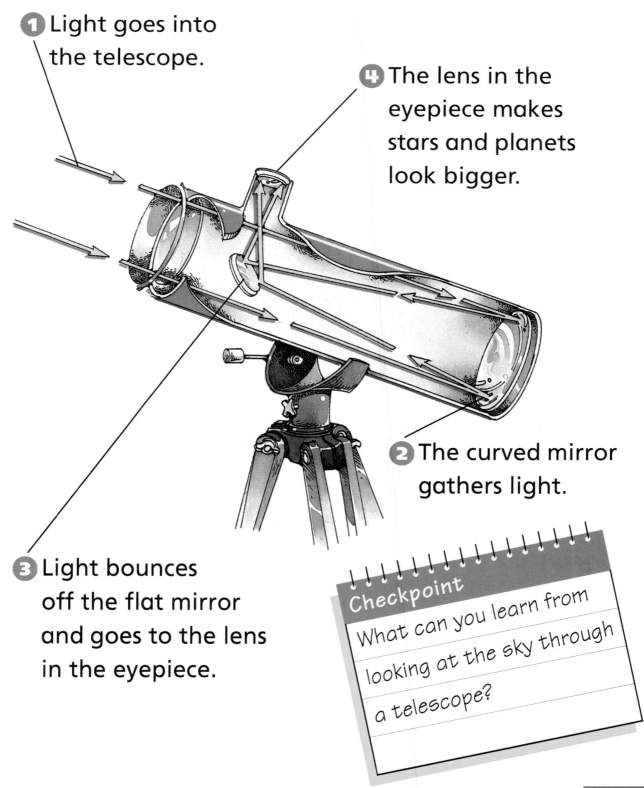

2 The curved mirror gathers light.

3 Light bounces off the flat mirror and goes to the lens in the eyepiece.

Checkpoint

What can you learn from looking at the sky through a telescope?

Show what you know.

Pretend you go on an imaginary trip. You travel to the moon, the sun, and other stars. You also visit different places on the earth. What do you see on your trip? What can you tell other people who want to take a trip like yours?

Plan your travel project.

1. Pick a project you would like to do.
2. How will you start your project?
3. How will your project look when you finish it?

Make travel posters.

Travel posters show places people can visit. Make travel posters about all the places you visited on your imaginary trip. Your posters can make people want to visit these places.

Talk with a reporter.

Pretend you are talking with a TV reporter. What questions can the reporter ask about all the places you visited on your imaginary trip. How can you answer the questions?

Write a travel guide.

Travel guides have words and pictures about places to visit. Make a travel guide about all the places you visited on your imaginary trip. Write about what people might see in these places.

Share what you know.

1. Share your project.
2. Which places would you like to visit? Why?
3. What part of your project did you like best?

Contents

Module A Living Things

Kids Did It 2-3
Study Guide 10-13
Experiment Skills 30-31

Module B Changes Over Time

Kids Did It 4-5
Study Guide 14-17
Experiment Skills 32-33

Module C Making Things Move

Kids Did It 6-7
Study Guide 18-21
Experiment Skills 34-35

Module D The Earth and Sky

Kids Did It 8-9
Study Guide 22-25
Experiment Skills 36-37

Using Scientific Methods 26-27
Safety in Science 28-29
Glossary/Index 38-46
Acknowledgments 47-48

Kids Are for the Birds

Birds don't have an easy life! They need lots of food to live. Our class wanted birds to find enough food in our schoolyard. So we decided to make bird feeders.

We worked in teams. First, we decided what kinds of birds would use our feeders. Next, we learned about the birds. We read about what they eat. We found out whether they need feeders with perches. We found out other things we needed to know.

Then we planned our feeders. They had to be the right size and shape for the birds. They had to hold the right kind of food. We also had to plan how to keep squirrels away.

Next, we made our bird feeders. When we were finished, we got together and shared them. It was fun to learn about different kinds of bird feeders. Finally, we put our bird feeders in different places around our school. Then we all became bird watchers!

You can do it.

Draw a picture of a bird feeder you would like to make. Tell about your bird feeder.

Kids Save the Earth

Our class thinks the earth is a beautiful place! So we think it's important to take care of the earth. We wanted to share ways to help the earth. So our class made up an alphabet game!

First, we each picked a letter of the alphabet. Then we made big paper letters. Next, we thought of a word that starts with our letter.

The word had to tell about a problem on the earth or a way to help the earth. Then we made a drawing about the word on our paper letter.

Finally, we all got together and shared our letters. We learned about ways to solve problems on the earth. Then we put our letters on our bulletin board. We invited other classes to see our ABC's About Our Earth. We were proud of what we had done!

You can do it.

Tell a friend about a problem on the earth. Talk about ways to solve the problem.

Kids Make It Move

Our teacher gave our class a problem to solve. We had to move a marble. The marble was on a table. We had to move the marble to a bowl on the floor. So we invented machines to help us move the marble.

First, each team made a plan for its invention. Next, we collected things we needed to build our machines. We collected cardboard tubes and boxes. We collected straws, paper cups, and many other things.

Then we built our machines and tested them. It was fun to watch how they worked! Finally our teams got together to share our inventions. Our class invented some very strange machines!

You can do it.

Invent a machine to move a marble. Share your invention with your classmates.

Kids Save Soil

Our new schoolyard was a dusty and muddy place to play. The ground was bare in some places. The soil in these places was blowing away. When it rained, the ground got muddy and soil washed away.

Our class wanted to help save the soil. So we made a map of the bare spots of land. Then we made a plan to take care of the bare land.

We found out that the roots of plants hold soil in the ground. Then the soil cannot be blown or washed away. So we decided to plant grass, flowers, and trees.

Each team picked a spot of land to care for. Our teams planted grass seeds and flower seeds. We planted flowers and trees. Soon colorful plants covered the bare ground.

You can do it.

Walk around your school or neighborhood. Find a place where the ground is bare. Tell what you could plant there.

Study Guide

Answer the questions. Use your own paper.

Chapter 1 Plants and Animals

A 4-5 1. Animals have special ____ parts.

leaf   body   floating

A 6-7 2. Look at the picture. What part does the butterfly use to smell flowers?

a. _____

b. _____

c. _____

A 8-9 3. Animals have ways of acting that help them ____ .

stay alive   stay cold   stay small

4. An animal hardly moves when it ____ .

flies   hibernates   eats

A 10-11 5. A brown caterpillar would be hard to see on a ____ leaf.

green   yellow   brown

A 12-13 6. A color or shape that makes an animal hard to see is called ____ .

nectar   red   camouflage

A 14-15 7. Plant ____ take in water from the soil.

leaves   roots   flowers

8. Look at the picture. Which plant parts make food the plant needs to live?

a. _____

b. _____

c. _____

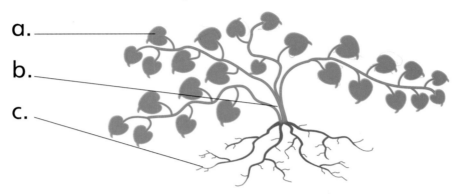

A 16-17 9. The thick ____ of the cactus hold water.

stems   leaves   seeds

A 18-19 10. Dandelion seeds are ____ through the air.

scattered   planted   grown

Chapter 2 Where Things Live

A 24-25 1. Plants and animals have special places where they ____ .

work   live   walk

A 26-27 2. Plants and animals live in many different kinds of ____ .

rocks   sunlight   habitats

A 28-29 3. A pond is one kind of ____ habitat.

dry   water   snowy

4. Green plants, ducks, and ____ might live in a pond habitat.

turtles   elephants   dogs

Study Guide

A 30-31 **5.** Animals get food, water, and _____ from their habitats.

insects   shelter   fur

6. A habitat gives plants _____ that they need to live.

nothing   some things   everything

A 32-33 **7.** Look at the pictures. Which of these is a good habitat for a cricket?

a.   b.   c.

A 34-35 **8.** Zoo habitats are built to give each kind of _____ everything it needs.

cage   animal   tree

A 36-37 **9.** Which of these is in a habitat for koalas?

a tree   an apple   a pond

Chapter 3 Grouping Living Things

A 42-43 **1.** You can _____ things by how the things are alike.

smell   group   float

A 44-45 **2.** A rock is a _____ thing.

living   growing   nonliving

3. Birds and grasses are kinds of _____ .
   plants   nonliving things   living things

A 46-47 4. Plants use _____ to make food they need.
   animals   habitats   sunlight

A 48-49 5. A turtle belongs to a group of animals
   called _____ .
   birds   fish   reptiles

6. Look at the pictures. Which animal
   belongs to a group called amphibians?
   a.   b.   c.

A 50-51 7. Animals with body hair or fur are _____ .
   turtles   mammals   fish

8. Birds have _____ on their bodies.
   feathers   scales   fur

A 52-53 9. A _____ is an animal with no legs.
   spider   worm   bee

10. Spiders have _____ legs.
   four   eight   six

11. Insects have _____ main body parts.
   three   six   eight

Study Guide

Answer the questions. Use your own paper.

Chapter 1 Discovering Dinosaurs

B 4-5   1. Dinosaurs lived in ____ on the earth.

   cities   many places   buildings

B 6-7   2. What size were dinosaurs?

   only big   big and small   only small

B 8-9   3. Could some dinosaurs fit in a space the size of your classroom?

   never   no   yes

B 10-11   4. Dinosaurs with long sharp teeth ate ____ .

   leaves   meat   flowers

5. Look at the pictures. Which kind of food did dinosaurs with big, flat teeth eat?

   a.   b.   c.

B 12-13   6. Dinosaur ____ tell how dinosaurs looked or acted.

   tails   names   teeth

7. What does the word dinosaur mean?

   big animal   terrible lizard   fast runner

B 14-15 **8.** Did all dinosaurs run fast?

always   yes   no

Chapter 2   Dinosaur Detectives

B 20-21 **1.** Looking at _____ can tell about a person.

questions   dinosaurs   objects

B 22-23 **2.** Dinosaurs left behind _____ .

buildings   footprints   mud

B 24-25 **3.** A _____ can be a part or mark from an animal or plant.

shell   fossil   tool

B 26-27 **4.** Look at the pictures. Which fossil came from a plant?

a.   b.   c.

B 28-29 **5.** Fossils are _____ rocks and dirt.

on top of   buried in   never found in

B 30-31 **6.** Some dinosaur bones became _____ .

mud   rocks   fossils

7. Dinosaur fossils tell us about _____ .

dinosaurs   people   plants

B 32-33 8. Dinosaur ____ can fit together like puzzle pieces fit together.

footprints   shapes   bones

B 34-35 9. Many fossils of dinosaur babies were found in ____ .

trees   nests   lakes

10. People learned about dinosaurs and their babies from studying ____ .

plants   mud   fossils

B 36-37 11. Fossils tell us about ____

long ago   people   puzzles

12. Look at the pictures. Which animal lived at the time of the dinosaurs?

a.   b.   c.

Chapter 3 A Changing World

B 42-43 1. The world is always ____ .

small   cold   changing

B 44-45 2. Kinds of animals are ____ when they no longer live on earth.

extinct   harmed   endangered

3. Which of these may have made dinosaurs become extinct?

fossils   people   cold weather

B 46-47 **4.** Plants and animals may not get what they need when their ____ change.

names   habitats   fossils

5. Kinds of plants and animals may become ____ if they cannot get what they need.

extinct   bigger   polluted

B 48-49 **6.** Kinds of plants and animals are ____ when only a few of them are still living on earth.

extinct   fossils   endangered

B 50-51 **7.** Polluted water is ____ water.

clean   dirty   safe

B 52-53 **8.** Smoke can make air become ____ .

polluted   fresh   clean

B 54-55 **9.** Look at the pictures. Which picture shows a way to help protect animals?

a.   b.   c.

Study Guide

Answer the questions. Use your own paper.

Chapter 1 How Things Move

C 4-5

1. A strong wind can make a sailboat _____ .

stay still   move   float

C 6-7

2. A push or a _____ is a force.

pull   turn   boat

3. You use _____ when you pull an object.

sound   light   force

C 8-9

4. Look at the pictures. Which picture shows a pull?

a.   b.   c.

C 10-11

5. Which push will make a ball roll farther?

strong push   weak push   no push

C 12-13

6. Which force will make a rubber band stretch the longest?

no force   weak force   strong force

C 14-15

7. It takes _____ force to move a heavy object than it does to move a light object.

less   more   weaker

8. Look at the pictures. Which pile of books would take the most force to move?

a.   b.   c.

C 16-17   **9.** It is easiest to pull a heavy box over a
_____ surface.

rough   bumpy   smooth

Chapter 2   Magnets

C 22-23   **1.** Two _____ can push and pull each other.

tables   metals   magnets

C 24-25   **2.** The ends of magnets are called north and south _____ .

poles   pushes   pulls

3. Two north poles held together will _____ .

push apart   pull together   not move

C 26-27   **4.** A magnet will pick up _____ .

a paper clip   an eraser   a paper

5. A magnet will not pick up _____ .

metal   paper clips   plastic

C 28-29   **6.** A _____ might have a magnet.

towel   toy   newspaper

C 30-31 7. A magnet can ____ through paper.

freeze   pull   bounce

C 32-33 8. A weak magnet will pick up ____ paper clips than a strong magnet.

more   heavier   fewer

C 34-35 9. A battery and a wire can turn a nail into a ____ .

magnet   hammer   paper clip

Chapter 3 Moving and Machines

C 40-41 1. You can find ways to move ____ in your classroom more easily.

trees   hammers   objects

C 42-43 2. A ____ makes work easier.

plant   machine   tree

3. Look at the pictures. Which picture shows a machine?

a.   b.   c.

C 44-45 4. A ____ can help you move a wheelchair.

hammer   ramp   skateboard

C 46-47 **5.** A _____ is a lever.

seesaw   wagon   ball bearing

C 48-49 **6.** Ball bearings can make it easier to _____ things.

smell   move   stretch

7. Which of these are like ball bearings?

marbles   blocks   ramps

C 50-51 **8.** When you drink milk, you use your arm like _____ .

a lever   a ramp   a ball bearing

9. Which of these body parts is like a machine?

a.   b.   c.

C 52-53 **10.** Your bones and muscles help you _____ .

learn   move   see

11. _____ in your body help you twist.

Joints   Arms   Bones

C 54-55 **12.** Bones and muscles work _____ .

alone   together   slowly

13. Muscles change _____ when bones move.

size   color   taste

Answer the questions. Use your own paper.

Chapter 1 The Sun

D 4-5 **1.** Night sky and day sky are _____ .

different   the same   both dark

D 6-7 **2.** The part of the earth that the sun is shining on has _____ .

nighttime   daytime   rain

D 8-9 **3.** The _____ is bigger than the earth.

sun   moon   cloud

D 10-11 **4.** The sun is made of hot _____ .

rocks   water   gases

D 12-13 **5.** Plants need _____ to grow.

darkness   sunlight   cold air

6. Look at the pictures. Which plant gets the sunlight it needs?

a.   b.   c.

D 14-15 **7.** Plants that animals eat need _____ to live and grow.

sunlight   clouds   moonlight

D 16-17 **8.** Energy that comes from the sun is called
_____ energy.

warm   fast   solar

D 18-19 **9.** Plants and animals that died long ago
changed into coal and _____ .

oil   air   water

Chapter 2 The Moon and Stars

D 24-25 **1.** Look at the pictures. Which picture shows
things you can see in the night sky?

a.   b.   c.

D 26-27 **2.** Some stars look small because they are
very _____ .

far away   close   dark

D 28-29 **3.** Long ago, people made up stories about
groups of _____ .

moons   stars   dots

D 30-31 **4.** Groups of stars that seem to form shapes
are called _____ .

animals   hunters   constellations

D 32-33 **5.** The moon has ____ light of its own.

 much   some   no

D 34-35 **6.** Look at the pictures. Which picture shows things that are on the moon?

 a.   b.   c.

7. The moon has many holes called ____ .

 craters   oceans   stars

D 36-37 **8.** The different shapes of the moon are called ____ .

 craters   phases   circles

9. The moon moves around the ____ .

 sun   earth   stars

Chapter 3 Looking at the Earth

D 42-43 **1.** You might dig through ____ when you dig in the earth.

 sand   hot gases   craters

D 44-45 **2.** You can find soil, and water on ____ .

 the stars   the sun   the earth

3. You can ____ rocks by color.

 count   group   measure

D 46-47 **4.** You can find water, ____ , and bits of rock in soil.

oceans   wind   air

D 48-49 **5.** Land is ____ the same everywhere on the earth.

almost   not   always

D 50-51 **6.** Most of the water on earth is in ____ .

rain   oceans   streams

7. Water on the ____ can be found in lakes, rivers, oceans, and streams.

earth   moon   sun

D 52-53 **8.** People cannot drink ocean water because it is ____ .

cold   warm   salty

D 54-55 **9.** Moving air is called ____ .

space   wind   rain

10. Look at the pictures. Which picture shows what wind can do?

a.   b.   c.

Almost every day scientists learn new things about the world. They try to find the answers to problems. Scientists use scientific methods to help them with problems. They use steps in their methods. Sometimes scientists use the steps in different order. You can use these steps to find answers too.

Explain the Problem

Ask a question like this. Does sun heat air?

Make Observations

Tell about the size, the color, or the shape of things.

Give a Hypothesis

Try to answer the problem. Think of different ideas. Then do an experiment to test your ideas.

Make a Chart or Graph

Write what you learn in your chart or your graph.

Make Conclusions

Decide if your hypothesis is right or wrong.

Safety in Science

Scientists are careful when they do experiments. You also need to be careful. Here are some safety rules to remember.

- Read each experiment carefully.

- Wear cover goggles when needed.

- Clean up spills right away.

- Never taste or smell unknown things.

- Do not shine lights in someone's eyes.

- Clean up when you finish an experiment.

- Wash your hands after each experiment.

Experiment with Crickets

Sam catches a cricket in the basement. He knows that crickets eat apples. He wonders if a cricket might eat meat too.

Problem

Do crickets eat meat?

Give Your Hypothesis

Answer the problem.
Then do the experiment.

Follow the Directions

1 Make a chart like this one.

day	food that is left
1	
2	

2 Put the cricket in a box with air holes.

3 Give the cricket a bit of meat, a bit of apple, and some water.

4 Check the food each day for 2 days.

5 In your chart, write what food is left each day.

day 1

day 2

Tell Your Conclusion

Do crickets eat meat?

Experiment with Fossils

The museum has more fossils of bones and teeth than other parts of dinosaurs. Rosa wonders if hard parts make better fossils than softer parts.

Problem

Do hard objects make better fossils than soft objects do?

Give Your Hypothesis

Answer the problem.
Then do the experiment.

Follow the Directions

1 Make a chart like this one.

what I used to make the fossils	what the fossils looked like
shell	
cotton ball	

2 Fill 2 paper cups half full of clay.

3 Put a small shell on the clay in 1 cup.

4 Put a cotton ball on the clay in the other cup. Fill both cups with plaster of Paris.

5 Let the plaster harden. Pull the cup and clay away from the plaster.

6 In your chart, draw how the fossils look.

Tell Your Conclusion

Do hard objects make better fossils?

Experiment with Magnets

Mary spills paper clips on the table. David offers to help pick them up. Mary wants to use a magnet. David thinks two magnets will make the job easier.

Problem

Are two magnets stronger than one?

Give Your Hypothesis

Answer the problem.
Then do the experiment.

Follow the Directions

1 Make a chart like this one.

number of magnets	number of clips
1	
2	

2 Put paper clips on the table.

3 Use 1 magnet to pick up the paper clips. How many do you pick up? Write the number in the chart.

4 Use 2 magnets to pick up the clips. How many do you pick up? Write the number in your chart.

Tell Your Conclusion

Are 2 magnets stronger than 1 magnet?

Experiment with the Sun and Heat

Dan wants to swim. His mother says the water is too cold. She tells Dan to swim later when the water is warm. Dan wonders if the sun heats the water.

Problem

Can the sun heat water?

Give Your Hypothesis

Answer the problem.
Then do the experiment.

Follow the Directions

1 Make a chart like this one.

water	temperature
cup in sun	
cup in shade	

2 Fill 2 cups with cold water.

3 Put 1 cup in a sunny place. Put the other cup in a shady place.

4 Wait for 2 hours.

5 Measure the temperature of each cup.

6 Write the temperatures in your chart. Circle the cup that has warmer water.

Tell Your Conclusion

Can the sun heat water?

A **amphibian,** p. A49. a group of animals that lives on land and in water. Frogs and toads are amphibians.

antenna, p. A7. one of the feelers on the heads of insects. The butterfly used its antennas to smell flowers.

B **ball bearings,** p. C48. balls that turn freely so that work is made easier. Ball bearings help the wheels of a car spin.

battery, p. C34. something that stores electricity. Large batteries make cars start.

bird, p. A49. a group of animals with wings, feathers, and two legs. Most birds can fly.

bone, p. C52. hard part of the body. Bones move when muscles pull them.

C **cactus,** p. A16. a plant that grows in hot dry places. A cactus grows in the desert.

camouflage, A12. color or shape of an animal that matches the place where the animal lives. A chipmunk's camouflage makes it hard to see in the woods.

caterpillar, p. A10. an insect that looks like a furry or colorful worm. A fuzzy caterpillar crawled on a branch.

clay, p. D42. soil that is easily shaped when wet and hard when dry. Bricks are made from clay.

coal, p. D18. a black rock that gives off heat when it is burned. Coal comes from plants that died millions of years ago.

constellation, p. D30. a group of stars that form a pattern. The Big Dipper is a constellation.

crater, p. D34. a hole in the ground shaped like a bowl. The surface of the moon is covered with craters.

cricket, p. A32. an insect that makes noise by rubbing its wings together. The cricket chirped all night.

D **desert,** p. A16. a dry habitat that is usually sandy and without trees. It was sunny and hot in the desert.

dinosaur, p. B4. animal that lived millions of years ago. I read a book about dinosaurs.

diorama, p. B36. a scene that shows a group of animals and plants against a modeled background. Joey's diorama of the desert looked so real.

E **electricity,** p. C34. a kind of energy. Electricity makes the lights work.

endangered, p. B48. might become extinct. We should protect endangered animals.

energy, p. D16. the power to do work. Light, heat, and electricity are kinds of energy.

extinct, p. B44. no longer lives on the earth. Dinosaurs are extinct.

F **fish,** p. A49. a group of animals covered with scales that live in water. I like to watch the fish swimming in the tank.

float, p. A18. to be held up by air, water, or other liquid. A hot air balloon will float in the sky.

force, p. C7. something that makes something else move. A push is a force.

fossil, p. B24. a part or a print of a plant or animal that lived long ago. She studied the dinosaur fossil.

fuel, p. D18. anything you can burn that gives heat or power. Wood is a fuel.

G **gas,** p. D10. something that is not solid or liquid and has no shape of its own. The air we breathe is made of several gases.

globe, p. D33. a small, round copy of the earth. A globe has a map of the earth drawn on it.

group, p. A42. to gather a number of persons or things together. The teachers grouped all the second graders together.

H **habitat,** p. A26. a place where living things live. The bird has a nest habitat.

hatch, p. B34. to come out from an egg. Two chickens hatched today.

hibernate, p. A9. spend the winter resting or sleeping. Bears hibernate all winter.

I insect, p. A30. a small animal with six legs and three body parts. Bees are insects.

J joint, p. C52. the place in the body where two bones are joined. Your knee is a joint.

K koala, p. A36. a small gray animal that looks like a bear. Koalas live in Australia.

L lever, p. C46. a bar used for lifting They used a lever to lift a rock.

living, p. A44. having life; something that grows. Animals and plants are two kinds of living things.

lizard, p. B12. a long, reptile. The lizard ran over my foot.

M machine, p. C42. something that applies force to make work easier. My new bicycle is a machine.

magnet, p. C22. something that pulls pieces of metal to it. Nails will stick to a magnet.

mammal, p. A49. a group of animals usually covered with hair or fur. Cats are mammals.

model, p. A54. a small copy of something. A globe is a model of the earth.

moon, p. D32. the brightest thing in the night sky. Sunlight shining on the moon makes it shine.

muscle, p. C52. a part of the body that helps the body move. Leg muscles help you run.

N **nectar,** p. A6. sweet liquid found in flowers. Bees make nectar into honey.

nonliving, p. A44. something that does not have life. A book is a nonliving thing.

O **oil,** p. D18. a thick liquid that comes from under the ground. Oil is a fuel.

P **phases,** p. D37. the shapes of the lighted part of the moon. Michi drew the different phases of the moon.

plant, p. A47. any living thing that can make its own food from sunlight, air, and water. Trees are plants.

pole, p. C24. the end of a magnet. Magnets have north and south poles.

polluted, p. B50. made dirty and harmful. The children couldn't swim in the lake because the water was polluted.

pond, p. A28. water with land all around it. A pond is smaller than a lake.

protect, p. B54. to keep something safe. Mother birds protect their babies.

R **ramp,** p. C44. a slope that connects two levels. I pushed the box up the ramp.

reptile, p. A49. a group of animals with dry, rough skin. Snakes are reptiles.

rot, p. B26. become spoiled. The apples started to rot.

rough, p. C18. an uneven surface, not smooth. Sandpaper feels rough.

scale, p. A50. the thin, hard pieces covering some fish, snakes and lizards. The scales on a fish are interesting.

scatter, p. A18. to throw a little bit here and there. The birds scattered the bird seed.

shell, p. B26. the hard, outside covering of some animals. Turtles have shells.

shelter, p. A30. something that covers something else from weather or danger. When it rained, everyone ran for shelter.

skeleton, p. B33. the bones of the body that support it and give it shape. You cannot see your skeleton.

smooth, p. C18. an even surface; not bumpy. The ice was so smooth that Bonnie was able to skate very fast.

soil, p. A27. dirt, the top layer of the earth. Marisa dug a small hole in the soil.

solar energy, p. D16. energy that comes from the sun. Many homes are heated with solar energy.

spider, p. A30. a very small animal with eight legs. I watched the spider spin its web.

star, p. D26. a tiny light in the night sky. A star is made up of hot, glowing gases.

stem, p. A14. the part of a plant that holds up leaves above the ground. The plant has a thin stem.

T

trunk, p. A15. the main stem of a tree. The children leaned against the trunk of the big oak tree.

V

valley, p D48. the low area between mountains or hills. Rivers often run through valleys.

W

web, p. A56. a net of tiny threads made by a spider. The spider's sticky web helps it catch its food.

wheel, p. C43. a kind of machine. Wheels help make a skateboard move easily.

wildlife, p. A38. plants or animals not grown or tamed by people. It is a good idea to have parks for wildlife.

Acknowledgments

ScottForesman

Editorial: Terry Flohr, Janet Helenthal, Carl Benoit, Mary Ann Mortellaro, Mary Jayne Horgan, Kathleen Lally, Marlene Joseph, Linda Roach, Pat Walsh

Art and Design: Barbara Schneider, Jacqueline Kolb

Picture Research/Photo Studio: Nina Page, Karen Koblik, John Moore, Phoebe Novak

Production: Barbara Albright, Francine Simon

Marketing: Ed Rock

Outside Credits
Interior Design
Kym Abrams Design, Inc.
The Quarasan Group, Inc.

Unless otherwise acknowledged, all photographs are the property of Scott, Foresman and Company. Page abbreviations are as follows: (T) top, (C) center, (B) bottom, (L) left, (R) right, (INS) inset.

Module A
Photographs
Front & Back Cover: Background: Patti Murray/EARTH SCENES Children's Photos: Michael Goss for Scott, Foresman and Company.

Page A2 John Shaw/Tom Stack & Associates **A3** Anna E.Zuckerman/Tom Stack & Associates **A5** Robert Lankinen/ The Wildlife Collection **A4(BL)** Don & Pat Valenti **A4(BR)** John Cancalosi/DRK Photo **A4-5(T)** Larry R.Ditto/Bruce Coleman, Inc. **A6** John Shaw/Tom Stack & Associates **A8-A9(T)** Jeff Foot/Bruce Coleman, Inc. **A8(B)** Mary Clay/ Tom Stack & Associates **A9(TR&B)** E.R.Degginger/ANIMALS ANIMALS **A12** Charlton Photographs **A13(T)** William E.Ferguson **A13(CL)** E.R.Degginger **A13(CR)** Marcia W.Griffen/ ANIMALS ANIMALS **A13(B)** Michael Fogden/DRK Photo **A14** Robert Frerck/Tony Stone Worldwide **A16** James Tallon **A18** David Cavagnaro/ Peter Arnold, Inc. **A24(L)** Tom Bean/DRK Photo **A24-A25(T)** Tom Bean/DRK Photo **A24-A25(B)** Margot Granitsas/The Image Works **A25(T)** Cameramann International Ltd. **A25(B)** Tom Bean/DRK Photo **A26-A27** Anna E.Zuckermann/Tom Stack & Associates **A28(T)** George I.Bernard/ANIMALS ANIMALS **A28(C)** Ray Richardson/ANIMALS ANIMALS **A28(B)** Ralph A.Reinhold/ANIMALS ANIMALS **A29(T)** Patti Murray/ANIMALS ANIMALS **A29(B)** E.R.Degginger **A34(T)** Rudi VonBriel **A34(B)-A35(B)** Esao Hashimoto/ANIMALS ANIMALS **A35(TL)** Ron Austing/Photo Researchers, Inc. **A36** Brian Parker/Tom Stack & Associates **A46(TL)** Aaron Haupt/David Frazier Photolibrary **A46(TR)** Stephen J.Krasemann/DRK Photo **A46(B)** Robert A.Tyrell/Oxford Scientific Films/ANIMALS ANIMALS **A47** John D.Cunningham/Visuals Unlimited **A50** Van Welsen/Tony Stone Worldwide **A52** David M.Dennis/Tom Stack & Associates **A53(TL)** E.R.Degginger **A53(R)** Hans Pfletschinger/Peter Arnold, Inc.

Illustrations
Page A7 Laurie O'Keefe **A15** Cindy Brodie **A20-21** Don Charles Meighan **A30-31** Erika Kors **A38-39** Nancy Lee Walter **A44-45** Renee Daily **A48-49** Kim Mulkey **A56-57** Don Charles Meighan **A61** Mike Eagle

Module B
Photographs
Front & Back Cover: Children's Photos: Michael Goss for Scott, Foresman and Company.

Page B2(T) Alex Kerstitch/Visuals Unlimited **B2(C)** Kjell B.Sandved/Visuals Unlimited **B20-B21(T) & B20(B)** Bruce Selyem/Museum of the Rockies, Montana State University **B21(TR)** Scott Berner/Visuals Unlimited **B21(C)** British Museum of Natural History **B21(BR)** Bruce Selyem/Museum of The Rockies, Montana State University **B26** William E.Ferguson **B27(T)** Alex Kerstitch/ Visuals Unlimited **B27(B)** Kjell B.Sandved/Visuals Unlimited **B28** Phil Degginger **B32** American Museum of Natural History, New York City Neg.2143 **B48(T)** Wendy Smith/Bob Rozinski/Tom Stack & Associates **B48(B)** Marty Stouffer/ ANIMALS ANIMALS **B49(TL)** Kerry T.Givens/Tom Stack & Associates **B49(TR)** William E.Ferguson **B49(B)** Gerald & Buff Corsi/Tom Stack & Associates **B56-B57** Gregory G.Dimijian, M.D./Photo Researchers, Inc. **B60** David R.Austen/Stock Boston

Illustrations
Page B2 Raymond E. Smith **B4-5** Robert Masheris **B6-7** Raymond E. Smith **B10** Ka Botzis **B12-13** Robert Masheris **B14-15** Cecile Duray-Bito **B16-17** Cecile Duray-Bito **B22** Ka Botzis **B30-31** Cecile Duray-Bito **B34-35** Ka Botzis **B36-37** Raymond E. Smith **B38-39** Sharron O'Neil **B42-43** Ronald C. Lipking **B44-45** Roberta Polfus **B46-47** Edward Brooks **B52** Rondi Collette **B61** Mike Eagle

Module C
Photographs
Front & Back Cover: Background: Holt Confer/DRK Photo Children's Photographs: Michael Goss for Scott, Foresman and Company.

Page C2(B) William E.Ferguson **C42** William E.Ferguson **C46** E.R.Degginger **C60** Courtesy, Huffy Bicycles

Illustrations
Page C4-5 Rondi Collette **C8-9** Yvette Banek **C18-19** Linda Hawkins **C28-29** Meryl Henderson **C36-37** Lisa Pompelli **C40-41** Cindy Brodie **C52-53** Vincent Perez **C57** Vincent Perez **C61** Mike Eagle

Module D
Photographs
Front & Back Cover: Background: E.R.Degginger   Children's
Photos: Michael Goss for Scott, Foresman and Company.

Page D3(B) Tom Bean/DRK Photo   **D4-D5** Joseph A.DiChello
D6-D7(T) Lawrence Migdale/Stock Boston
D6-D7(B) Mike J.Howell/Stock Boston   **D10** NASA
D16 Bob Daemmrich/Stock Boston   **D26-D27** Dennis DiCicco
D32 E.R.Degginger   **D34** NASA   **D36-D37** Dennis DiCicco
D48 Stephen J.Krasemann/DRK Photo   **D49** Tom Bean/DRK Photo
D50-D51(T) Telegraph Colour Library/FPG
D50-D51(B) Larry Ulrich/DRK Photo
D51(TR) Scott Berner/Visuals Unlimited
D51(BR) Stan Osolinski/Tony Stone Worldwide
D60 Alan Carey/The Image Works

Illustrations
Page D3 Pam Hohman   **D14-15** Rondi Collette
D18-19 Raymond E. Smith   **D20-21** Lisa Pompelli
D24-25 Diana Philbrook   **D28-29** Pam Hohman
D38-39 Nan Brooks   **D56-57** Linda Hawkins
D61 Mike Eagle

Back Matter
Photographs
Page 9 Bob Daemmrich/The Image Works
Illustrations
Pages 10-25, 38-46 Precision Graphics